Praise for
Joy to the World

"There are many reasons that we love the celebration of Christmas, but two stand out: it is a time for joy and it is a time for family. We rejoice in the birth of Jesus Christ and the salvation He came to bring us, and we take time to be with our families during this special season. In this wonderful book, Scott Hahn beautifully explains that the Christmas story is foremost a family story. You will learn about the deep Scriptural meaning of the Nativity of Jesus Christ and come to more fully appreciate the unique role played by the figures we know so well from the Gospels' accounts. From Mary and Joseph to the Magi and shepherds, this book will help you discover anew the joy of Christmas!"

—Cardinal Timothy M. Dolan, Archbishop of New York

"Scott Hahn crosses 'boundaries' that are sometimes used to separate history from Scripture and both from doctrine in order to give us a more adequate grasp of the boundaries God has crossed in the mystery of the Incarnation. This book is a joy to read and to ponder."

—Francis Cardinal George, O.M.I., Archbishop of Chicago and author of *God in Action*

"Let Christmas come alive this year! With the help of his daughter, Hannah, who accompanied him to Bethlehem, Scott Hahn sees beyond the category of 'only for children' storytelling to provide a narrative for people of all ages about the day the Word became flesh—the birth of Jesus. *Joy to the World: How Christ's Coming Changed Everything (and Still Does)* is great Christmas reading, especially for families."

—Most Reverend Joseph E. Kurtz, D.D., Archbishop of Louisville and president of the United States Conference of Catholic Bishops

"I greatly enjoyed reading Scott Hahn's *Joy to the World*. In a spirit of joyful discipleship and with his command of Scripture, he leads us step by step into the heart of God's plan for the world's salvation and thus into the heart of the New Evangelization. What a wonderful resource for those seeking to deepen their discipleship and those seeking truth and love in their lives."

—Most Reverend William E. Lori, Archbishop of Baltimore

"Let Scott Hahn, one of Catholicism's most talented biblical scholars, take you more deeply into the Christmas story. In a work both scholarly and accessible, he answers the most common questions about the story of Jesus's birth, 'opens up' some all-important Gospel passages, and overall, helps us understand why the birth of a poor child 2,000 years ago has the power to change our lives today."
—James Martin, SJ, author of *Jesus: A Pilgrimage*

"Scott Hahn welcomes the reader to see various levels of the importance of Christmas, using new developments in scholarship that move the reader away from cheap and easy skepticism toward the abundant data from Scripture, Jewish sources, and pagan historians. While skeptics consider it an accomplishment to question the Bible in order to make you doubt, Hahn leads readers to think carefully, meditate more profoundly, pray more earnestly, and discover joy in the world."
—Mitch Pacwa, SJ, author of *How to Listen When God Is Speaking*

"The danger of the familiar is that we can walk all our lives right past that which God has given to draw us closer to Him. In *Joy to the World*, Scott Hahn helps us slow down and rediscover, as if for the first time, the life-changing gift of Christmas through the lens of the family."
—Marcus Grodi, president of the Coming Home Network

"Pope Francis says we can't have pickled pepper Christians. Instead it is our joy that will attract people to the Church. In *Joy to the World*, Scott helps us get closer to the source of that joy with a beautiful journey through time and history, a journey taking us back to where it all began. This book reminds us that Christmas should be celebrated in our hearts all year long. Joy to the world indeed."
—Teresa Tomeo, author of *God's Bucket List*

"In the Incarnation of the Word made flesh, joy entered the world at Christmas and continues its merry invasion of our darkness with each celebration of the Eucharist. Dr. Scott Hahn, with his customary blend of biblical erudition, plain English, and heartfelt love for Jesus Christ is a glad herald, a deep thinker, an accessible teacher, and a loving guide into this profound and happy mystery. May his tribe increase!"
—Mark P. Shea, author of *By What Authority?: An Evangelical Discovers Catholic Tradition*

JOY
TO THE
WORLD

ALSO BY SCOTT HAHN

*Angels and Saints: A Biblical Guide to Friendship
with God's Holy Ones*

*Consuming the Word: The New Testament and the
Eucharist in the Early Church*

The Lamb's Supper: The Mass as Heaven on Earth

Hail, Holy Queen: The Mother of God in the Word of God

First Comes Love: Finding Your Family in the Church and the Trinity

Lord, Have Mercy: The Healing Power of Confession

Swear to God: The Promise and Power of the Sacraments

Letter and Spirit: From Written Text to Living Word in the Liturgy

*Reasons to Believe: How to Understand, Explain, and
Defend the Catholic Faith*

*Ordinary Work, Extraordinary Grace:
My Spiritual Journey in Opus Dei*

Understanding the Scriptures: A Complete Course on Bible Study

*Understanding "Our Father":
Biblical Reflections on the Lord's Prayer*

A Father Who Keeps His Promise: God's Covenant Love in Scripture

Rome Sweet Home: Our Journey to Catholicism with Kimberly Hahn

*Living the Mysteries: A Guide for
Unfinished Christians* with Mike Aquilina

Signs of Life: 40 Catholic Customs and Their Biblical Roots

Many Are Called: Rediscovering the Glory of the Priesthood

Catholic Bible Dictionary, General Editor

JOY
TO THE
WORLD

How Christ's Coming
Changed Everything
(and Still Does)

Scott Hahn

IMAGE

NEW YORK

Published in the United States by Image, an imprint of
the Crown Publishing Group, a division of Random House LLC, New
York, a Penguin Random House Company.
www.crownpublishing.com

IMAGE is a registered trademark and the "I" colophon is a trademark of
Random House LLC.

Library of Congress Cataloging-in-Publication Data

Hahn, Scott.
Joy to the world : how Christ's coming changed everything (and still does) /
Scott Hahn. — First Edition.
pages cm
Includes bibliographical references.
1. Christmas—Meditations. 2. Jesus Christ—Nativity—Meditations.
3. Catholic Church—Doctrines. I. Title.
BV45.H28 2014
232.92—dc23
2014034025

ISBN 978-0-8041-4112-3
eBook ISBN 978-0-8041-4113-0

PRINTED IN THE UNITED STATES OF AMERICA

Book design by Ellen Cipriano
Jacket design by Jessie Sayward Bright
Jacket art: Bridgeman Art Library
Author photograph: Trace Murphy

3   5   7   9   10   8   6   4

First Edition

To Holy Mary, cause of our joy

(Luke 1:39–45)

The history of salvation is not a small event, on a poor planet, in the immensity of the universe. It is not a minimal thing which happens by chance on a lost planet. It is the motive for everything, the motive for creation. Everything is created so that this story can exist, the encounter between God and his creature.

—Pope Benedict XVI, address at the opening of the
12th Ordinary General Assembly of the
Synod of Bishops, October 6, 2008

CONTENTS

JOY
TO THE
WORLD

CHAPTER

1

A LIGHT GOES ON IN BETHLEHEM

*I*T WAS EARLY SPRING. Christmas was more than half a year away, but the crowd of pilgrims around us sang "O Little Town of Bethlehem" and "O Come, All Ye Faithful." That's the year-round custom at the Holy Land's Basilica of the Nativity.

O come ye, O come ye to Bethlehem!

As many as two million visitors pass through the little town every year. Almost all arrive as pilgrims to venerate—or tourists to gawk at—the place where Jesus was born. They stand in long lines to pause for a brief moment before the site where Mary and Joseph took shelter and the field where angels announced the birth to shepherds. There is time for a quick prayer, perhaps, before the monk who serves as custodian urges you to make way for the next person in line.

To the intensely devout or the intensely curious, a moment

1

is enough. It's worth the occasional anti-Christian slur called at you in a city that is now predominantly Muslim. It's worth the hostilities you might have to witness in a city that has been a combat zone in recent memory. (The Basilica of the Nativity was occupied and besieged in 2002.) It's certainly worth the inconvenience of the wait in line.

The sense of effort and danger is part of Bethlehem's appeal for pilgrims like me. So I felt exhilarated as my family moved from site to site. I strained to hear every whispered word of the tour guides, who were hushed by monks whenever they dared to raise their voices. As I waited in line I scanned the walls and the horizon in search of small details I might know from Scripture and history.

Amid my reveries, though, my roving eyes were drawn again and again to a more familiar sight: my dear and only daughter, my twelve-year-old, Hannah. She looked bored and restless.

The devotion of an older generation can seem an alien thing to a teen. Hannah knew the Bible stories, of course, but not in the way I knew them—from the years I had spent in seminary and then in a doctoral program in theology. I could see that the guides who enthralled me bored her, as they droned on about the distant past. And she seemed less than satisfied by the reward at the end of a long wait in line: a few seconds to stretch gymnastically in order to kiss some holy and historic rock.

By the time we reached Bethlehem, we had already visited several other biblical sites, and the strain was showing on Hannah's face. I tried to give her extra attention, at the Basilica of the Nativity, to ease the time in line for the crypt.

Our group passing through was very large, hundreds of people from several buses, but Hannah and I were among the first to queue up, so we soon found ourselves descending the short staircase into the crypt under the church's main altar—the cave where, according to ancient tradition, the Blessed Virgin Mary gave birth to Jesus.

We paused and prayed and bent low to kiss the fourteen-point silver star that marks the spot.

As we emerged from the exit staircase, we could see the line from our group—now stretched the length of the basilica and out the doors in back. I told Hannah it could be an hour's wait till all our people made it through. It was probably not the most helpful thing to say. She sighed a deep teenaged sigh, expressing a boredom that approached despair, and I prayed the usual parental prayer for wisdom.

Then came the godsend.

One of the local people who were working with our group came over to announce the next scheduled stop: our group would pay a visit to a nearby orphanage. We could begin moving in that direction.

I looked at Hannah, and her face lit up. The orphanage trip meant immediate release from the dim church where she'd been doomed to the slow counting of tourists who passed by.

Our guide led us out the doors and into the bright sunlight of the square. It was a quick walk to the orphanage, and we had no trouble keeping the pace. Even I felt relieved after the slow shuffle of the queues. And Hannah seemed more engaged than she had at any other moment since our arrival in the Holy Land.

The orphanage was crowded with children, but they were bright and clean. Hannah was giddy, practically ecstatic, to be around children instead of monuments. She did not know, and maybe could not understand, the reason such a place was necessary. She knew little about the Israeli-Palestinian conflicts—the bombs, the battles, the economic collapse, and the primitive medical care that had left so many children without the care of a mother and father.

The little boys and girls beamed as they saw Hannah and closed in for her company. In early adolescence, she was a giant among the toddlers, yet she was clearly *not* a grown-up. Her age accommodated her perfectly to their care. The staff at the orphanage led her to a chair and asked if she would like to hold babies. Hannah smiled and gave an eager yes. It was important, they explained, that each infant receive a healthy amount of close human contact every day—the closeness they would get in a home with parents and siblings.

The third of six children, Hannah had had long experience

with babies. So she knew what to do when a nurse handed her the first bundle. She cradled the tiny boy in her arms and leaned her face down toward his. Her voice rose an octave as she lavished endearments on him.

She must have made all the right moves. A caretaker came to cycle that baby out—and replace him with another. And then another.

Hannah beamed. She was animated in a way she had not been since we left home. She chattered with us cheerily between coos for the baby.

I was feeling happy because she was feeling happy—and then I got hit by another sort of happiness.

As I watched Hannah, radiant in that chair in Bethlehem, I thought of another teenaged girl. She, too, had come to this town from far away. Her eighty-mile journey by donkey surely took longer than our nonstop flight from New York. She arrived under circumstances that were less than ideal. She surely had to wait in line and deal with crowds. Sleepy first-century Bethlehem was not designed to handle a census.

Yet that young woman, long centuries ago, found fulfillment in Bethlehem—in a baby placed in her arms. Everyone who saw her remembered her radiance, and after two thousand years we still remember it.

Looking at Hannah as she looked at those babies, I could understand why.

The effect on Hannah was long-lasting. She was

changed—visibly changed and inwardly transformed. You could see it in her face and in her deeds. Months later, she organized a fund-raiser to send clothes to "her orphans" in Bethlehem. She had undergone a spiritual awakening, but still more than that. It was a kind of *maternal* awakening—a coming of age—a transition from *being* a little kid to *caring* for little kids.

There were many wonderful memories from that trip, but our time in the orphanage stood out. In Bethlehem I know I saw the joy of Christmas—not exactly at the spot of the nativity, but not far from it.

What had been merely a word for me—Christmas—was now a word made flesh. And the moment is still vivid in my memory. The reality of Christmas, for me, is not primarily what I learned at seminary or in the research I slogged through in pursuit of a doctorate. Christmas is, for me, the joy and the love that passed between a young woman and the child who had been placed in her arms.

That child was Jesus, and in time he made way for another child who needed love—and that child was you—and that child was me. He grew and redeemed us so that he could welcome us into the life he lived here on earth. He welcomed us into the very family he created for himself.

Jesus did not come into this world alone. He came into this world by way of a family, and he brought us salvation so that we could share membership in the family of God. That's the very meaning of salvation and the meaning of Christmas: "But to all who received him, who believed in his name, he gave power to become *children of God*" (John 1:12)—God's sons and daughters, members of his family. If we don't understand Christmas, then we don't really understand what Jesus did when he saved us. There is a family dimension to all the saving mysteries—from the Lord's passion and death to his institution of the sacraments and the Church—but nowhere is it so brilliantly manifest as in the story of the birth of Jesus.

That's what my daughter, Hannah, showed me in Bethlehem all those years ago.

The Christmas story is one of the most popular stories in all of history, yet I would argue that it defies many of the conventions of narrative. The most enduring stories are usually those that have outstanding heroes and memorable villains.

Christmas does have its villains, and they're easy to identify. Bloodthirsty King Herod looms over the opening chapter of Saint Matthew's Gospel. When Saint John speaks symbolically about the Messiah's birth, in Revelation 12, he informs us that the real archvillain is Satan himself, portrayed as a murderous dragon.

But who is the hero of the Christmas story? We tend to read the Gospel narrative through two millennia of tradition, and so the answer seems obvious: The hero is Jesus! He's the "reason for the season." He's the Christ we strive to keep in *Christ*-mas. It's his story we hear and then go out to "tell it on the mountain."

Yes, Jesus is at the center of the drama, but he doesn't behave like a conventional hero. He doesn't fit the classical model. He's not acting alone. He's not intruding himself to change the course of events. In fact, he's hardly *acting* at all. He's passive: nursed and placed to sleep in a manger, found on his mother's lap by the Magi, carried away in flight to Egypt. Like any baby, he exercises a powerful attraction—drawing love from those who draw near. Yet he is visible only because other arms are holding him.

The Christmas story has an unconventional hero—not a warrior, not a worldly conqueror, not an individual at all, but rather a *family*. The details of the story always lead us back to that fact. We see the swaddling bands and know they're for a baby, but *someone* had to do the swaddling. So we have a mother and child. We have a father. We have a household. We hear tell of the manger-crib where he lay, but *someone* needed to place him there. We read of the child's exile in Egypt, but *someone* had to take him there—someone had to protect him from brigands along the desert roads—and someone had to work hard to support the mother and baby in a foreign land.

The scenes of Jesus's early life—Mary's crisis pregnancy,

Joseph's provident decisions, Herod's persecution—are dramatic precisely because they involve the intersection of so many individual lives. Indeed, the other details of the story derive their meaning from the Gospel's primary focus on the family: the Holy Family. The evil king Herod is clearly *anti*-family, *anti*-child—murdering Bethlehem's offspring, devouring them. History tells us that King Herod slaughtered *his own sons,* and the Gospel shows him commanding his soldiers to turn their swords upon the children of Bethlehem.

The family is the key to Christmas. The family is the key to Christianity. Pope Saint John Paul II noted that everything good—history, humanity, salvation—"passes by way of the family."[1] When God came to save us, he made salvation inseparable from family life, manifest in family life. Since the family is the ordinary setting of human life, he came to share it, redeem it, and perfect it. He made it an image and sacrament of a divine mystery. Salvation itself finds meaning only in *familial* relations.

The truth of Christmas begins with a family. The events turned historically on the decisions of a husband and father, a wife and mother. We know of these events only because that mother pondered them in her heart and chose to share them with her son's disciples (Luke 2:19, 51).

The truth of Christmas was passed on by way of families. Ancient pilgrims found their way to the cave of the nativity, not because there were historical markers and directional signs along the dirt roads of Bethlehem, but because the earliest Christians—some of them perhaps eyewitnesses, or the children of eyewitnesses—had pondered the local events and passed on their accounts to the next generations.

For centuries, their faith was illegal. In Bethlehem, as elsewhere, they met for worship not in grand churches, but in family homes. And they considered all who met together to be one common family. That, indeed, is one of the most profound implications of the Christmas story: that God had made his dwelling place among men, women, and children, and he called them—he calls us—to become his family, his holy household.

That, then, is the theme of the chapters that follow. They are meditations on Christ's coming into the world—the Christmas story—in light of its most intimate and most necessary historical setting. We'll meet the members of the Holy Family and join them on their journeys: to Bethlehem, to Jerusalem, and to Egypt. We'll consider the deepest meaning of the small details of the narrative: the angels and the manger, the swaddling bands and the Magi, the star and the shepherds. The details sometimes seem strange and impenetrable until we consider them in relation to a home, a mother, a father, a bond, a household, a lineage, a heritage.

And now the heritage is ours! We are Christ's family, and

so the joy of Christmas belongs to us. And it can be experienced not just in the Holy Land, but anywhere, at any time of year, every day. Without Christ, the world was a joyless place; and anyplace where he remains unknown and unaccepted is a joyless place. Everything has changed since Christ's birth, yet everything remains to be changed, as people come to receive the child in faith.

CHAPTER

2

WHAT HAPPENS IN BETHLEHEM . . .

*A*S I PREPARED THE first chapter of this book, I had
to dig deep in my memory. I was able also to consult
other resources to corroborate details. In fact, I called Hannah
on the phone. (She's now flourishing as a wife and mother.)
She remembered everything well because her experience at
the orphanage in Bethlehem had been transformative for her.
She had returned from that trip and immediately organized a
fund-raiser for her beloved orphans in Bethlehem.

What happens in Bethlehem doesn't stay in Bethlehem. It
goes home with pilgrims. That was certainly true of the Holy
Family. "Mary kept all these things, pondering them in her
heart" (Luke 2:19).

With those words Luke the evangelist ends his narrative
of Jesus's conception, birth, and infancy. A few paragraphs

later he concludes his account of Jesus's later childhood with a variation on the same theme, noting, "his mother kept all these things in her heart" (2:51). Commentators since ancient times have concluded that both "heart" lines were simply the evangelist's way of citing the Blessed Virgin as his firsthand source.

For Luke was a scrupulous historian, attentive to detail and much concerned about getting his facts straight. Alone among the evangelists, he uses precise medical and anatomical terms when he describes Jesus's miraculous cures. And he is careful to place events accurately in terms of time and place. He tells us that the census that drew the Holy Family to Bethlehem was "the first enrollment, when Quirinius was governor of Syria" (Luke 2:2). He would not have it confused with any other, similar event. Mary and Joseph, he continues, "went up from Galilee, from the city of Nazareth, to Judea, to the city of David, which is called Bethlehem" (Luke 2:4). Times and places matter to him because he is passing on what he has received from eyewitness testimony.

The Blessed Virgin was the only person who *could* have given eyewitness accounts of the unusual events surrounding the first Noel—the angelic visitations; the journeys from Nazareth to "the hill country," to Bethlehem, and to Jerusalem; the private conversations at the Temple; not to mention a birth hidden away in a stable. Mary was, moreover, the only person who could have given an account of her own interior response to these marvels.

Mary is the only possible witness to Jesus's conception and birth. And Luke is a credible witness to Mary's "pondering." Reliable tradition places the Blessed Virgin in Ephesus with the apostle John (see John 19:26–27) in the decades after Jesus's ascension into heaven. Luke also traveled there, and chapter 19 of his Acts of the Apostles shows his familiarity with the region. He uses, for example, the peculiar local terms for offices and assemblies of city life, and these are confirmed by other contemporary and local sources. It's unlikely that such a careful historian—and so devout a Christian—would have traveled so close to the Mother of the Lord and never sought an interview.

He recorded what she had for many years "pondered . . . in her heart," and he reported her reflections in passages that seem understated, given the extraordinary events they describe.

Such simplicity and understatement are hallmarks of the earliest Christian testimonies and traditions. These qualities set the canonical Gospels apart from later, noncanonical writings. There are other "gospels"—other documents that purport to tell the story of Jesus's infancy—but the narratives in the apocrypha concern themselves mostly with spectacle and power. They worry overmuch about what skeptics might say.

Their style is overexcited and bombastic. They transgress good taste and strain credulity beyond the breaking point. They provide entirely too much information about medical aspects of Mary's birth.

Luke, on the other hand, like Matthew, manages to convey marvels in a matter-of-fact tone. The canonical accounts are the fruit of long years of quiet reflection. They have been pondered in the loving hearts of eyewitnesses and distilled to their essence.

The stories of Jesus's birth, as we find them in the New Testament, are corroborated—in spirit as well as in the details—by many of the earliest local traditions. The memories pondered by Jesus's mother were shared with the Church and "kept in the family" as a heritage.

The primary witnesses to Christmas are the accounts of Matthew and Luke. They were written as history, though for two different audiences, each with its own culture and conventions for preserving history. Matthew, the early records tell us, wrote originally in Hebrew for a Jewish-Christian audience. Luke wrote for Greek-speaking Gentiles and Jews.

In the course of our discussion we'll spend most of our time in those Gospel pages. Occasionally though we'll gain insight from other New Testament books. We have much to learn from tradition as well, and from archaeology, and from the writings of the early Church Fathers. Most Christians, sad to say, know little about the earliest accounts of Christmas (apart from those in the Bible).

Consider, for example, the evidence we find in the writings of Saint Justin Martyr. He was born around AD 100 to a pagan family in Flavia Neapolis (today called Nablus), some forty miles north of Bethlehem. He knew the people and the area quite well, and he knew the site of "a certain cave"[1] that the locals venerated as the place of Jesus's birth—even at that early date. He doesn't dwell on the fact. He simply mentions in passing that local Christians took care to preserve the historical memory of the nativity.

In the century after Justin's account, a great Egyptian scholar named Origen made his own pilgrimage to Bethlehem, and he wrote his own account of the visit—in response to the scorn of a hostile skeptic. "At Bethlehem the cave is shown where he was born, and the manger in the cave where he was wrapped in swaddling-clothes. And this sight is greatly talked about in surrounding places, even among the enemies of the faith. They say that *in this cave* Jesus was born, who is worshipped and reverenced by the Christians."[2]

It is not just a cave, but *"this* cave," a certain cave. For Origen, as for the evangelists before him and for Justin, there is a verifiable particularity about the facts of Jesus's conception, birth, and infancy. These events happened not "once upon a time," but "in the days of Herod, king of Judea," when "a decree went out from Caesar Augustus" (Luke 1:5; 2:1).

The history of Christianity begins with the story of Christmas. And it is history—not myth, fable, or folklore. The canonical accounts fit none of those literary genres.

The evangelists worked with great economy, guided by the Holy Spirit, and preserved only what was essential. The Gospels tell us little about Jesus's early life except a few episodes. Yet each of the few small details we have is freighted with saving truth. Those are the details caringly pondered by the Virgin and carefully reported by the evangelists.

The stories of Jesus's conception and birth are certainly unusual. They recount several apparitions of angels, unique astronomical phenomena, and no shortage of miracles. Modern readers, by training, are not sure what to do with all this. We live in a world of marvels, but we are schooled to put these aside if they do not fit the broadest generalities in categories confirmed by the scientific method and approved by a magisterium of skeptics.

In the third volume of his masterwork, *Jesus of Nazareth*, Pope Benedict XVI considers the infancy narratives and asks the inevitable question: "Are we dealing with history that actually took place, or is it merely a theological meditation, presented under the guise of stories?"[3]

Since the eighteenth century, a dominating group of scholars—some professing to be Christian and others not—have asked the same question and answered it in the negative. They have argued that the infancy narratives (and other stories of the miraculous) preserve something other than historical data. Some say the infancy narratives are myths modeled on those of other world religions—or allegories, following the literature of the Greeks. Others say they are "haggadic midrash," a form of illustrative tale, purposefully fanciful, crafted to make a doctrinal point. Still others claim the infancy narratives are simply fables with a useful moral purpose, like those of Aesop.

Pope Benedict examined these approaches carefully and fairly, but ultimately he rejected them as interpretive keys to the biblical narratives of Jesus's birth. Theology and history, he explained, are not mutually exclusive (or contradictory) categories. If God exists, he is the Lord of History, and history cannot be reduced to the accumulation of political, economic, and military data. If God exists, then his purposes may be fulfilled in families as much as in armies. His purposes may be fulfilled *as we see them fulfilled* in the family of Israel in the Old Testament and the family of the Church in the New Testament.

Pope Benedict concluded: "The infancy narratives are not a meditation presented under the guise of stories, but the converse: Matthew is recounting real history, theologically thought through and interpreted, and thus he helps us to understand the mystery of Jesus more deeply."[4] The Holy Father noted, moreover, that scholarly opinion has shifted subtly in this direction for the last half-century.

In this book I pick up the same assumptions that engaged Pope Benedict, though my concerns are substantially different from his. When we read of the birth of the Messiah, we are dealing not in myths, legends, or folktales, Pope Benedict wrote: "What Matthew and Luke set out to do, each in his own way, was not to tell 'stories' but to write history, real history that had actually happened, admittedly interpreted and understood in the context of the word of God."[5]

Though the Gospel is certainly rich in allegorical meaning, it is first of all *history*. If there is allegory in the infancy narratives, it is fashioned by God, and not simply with words, but rather with creation itself—with the very deeds of sacred history. God writes the world the way human authors write words. Spiritual truths are everywhere to be found in the events at the beginning of the Gospels, but the events are nonetheless real and nonetheless important. They are no less historical for being extraordinary. To invoke Pope Benedict again: "If God does not also have power over matter, then he simply is not God. But he does have this power."[6] And so he can (and has) guided history and creation, just as he guided the prophets, to tell his story.

Pope Francis put the matter with characteristic bluntness: "The birth of Jesus is not a fairy tale! It is the story of a real event, which occurred in Bethlehem two thousand years ago."[7] It is history—our family history—carefully kept and passed down in the household we call the Church, to bring joy to every generation.

The events of Christmas challenge us, just as they challenged the original characters—the *family*—whose history they tell.

❧

A NEW GENESIS

*T*HE *NEW TESTAMENT BEGINS* not with a discourse or a prophecy, not with theology or law, but with a simple declaration of family relationships.

> The book of the genealogy of Jesus Christ, the son of David, the son of Abraham. (Matthew 1:1)

Matthew began his proclamation of the Gospel in the most deliberate way, with a succinct statement of his theme and purpose. It's not even a complete sentence. It was almost certainly intended to serve as a title for the lines that follow and perhaps for the entire Gospel.

And what a loaded title it is. In that brief, functional fragment is the meaning of Christmas and of Christianity.

Biblos geneseos, begins the Greek, and those two words

pack suggestive power. *Geneseos* can mean "genealogy," as it is usually translated into English, but it can also mean "beginning" or "origin." From the root *geneseos* we English speakers get the *genes* that make us who we are. We get the *genome* whose map tells us of our ancestors and their peculiar traits. We speak of the *generations* down our family line.

Saint Matthew's first readers knew nothing of the field of genetics, but the title spoke still more loudly to them. To those first readers, the evangelist was suggesting a new Genesis, an account of the new creation brought about by Jesus Christ. In the fourth Gospel, Saint John accomplishes something similar when he begins by echoing the first words of the Torah: "In the beginning" (John 1:1; see Genesis 1:1). Saint Matthew introduces the same theme, though in a different way. The message in both is clear: with the arrival of Jesus, God brings about a new beginning, a new creation, a new Torah, and a New Testament.

And the form it takes is familial. Matthew traces the history of salvation not by way of epic battles and conquests—and certainly not by way of influential ideas—but by way of family. He names Israel's long-expected Anointed One, the *Christ,* and identifies him primarily as a "son," the offspring of a particular family. Jesus is thus defined by his relations of kinship—with David, with Abraham, and ultimately with God.

❧

To modern readers, the Gospel genealogies can seem tedious to the point of absurdity. It's often painful when they come up in the readings for Mass, and parish priests must struggle through the long lists of unfamiliar and unpronounceable names.

It seems an inscrutable mystery why the Church would begin its sacred book with something so boring. Is it simply an act of defiance? Is Matthew daring us to wade through a purgatorial swamp of ancient trivia before we enjoy the glories of Christmas?

The answer is an absolute no. Matthew began his Gospel with the most compelling, exciting, and relevant material he had at hand.

Matthew crafted his narrative to appeal to Jews. They were a people with a common ancestry. They traced themselves back to Abraham, through his son Isaac and grandson Jacob (also known as Israel), and they found their place in the twelve tribes descended from Jacob's sons. Most of the tribes had been dispersed or lost, but members of the tribe of Judah repeatedly found their way back to the land promised to Abraham by God. With their sense of common ancestry came a sense of shared inheritance, homeland, birthright, history, and destiny.

And their history was the key to understanding their

destiny. Israel had been enslaved and had suffered conquest, exile, dispersion, and profanation. Yet God had always delivered them. This was the story they were raised to remember, and even after many centuries of hard times, the people of Israel knew it was *their* story. It was not something foreign or strange in any way. They themselves were caught up in it, and they anxiously awaited a decisive resolution of their troubles.

Each name in Matthew's genealogy would have suggested a dramatic episode—or many episodes—in Israel's history. It was a story they knew well.

Immediately, with his first line Matthew places Jesus in the line of his nation's most illustrious men. As Son of David and Son of Abraham, he was heir to the throne, the kingship of Israel.

Who was David? Who was Abraham?

Abraham was the patriarch of Israel. Around 2000 BC, God called him away from his homeland of Mesopotamia— away from idolatry—to be the father of a nation that would be distinguished by its worship of the one true God. God promised to bless Abraham in his progeny: "Kings shall come forth from you. And I will establish my covenant between me and you and your descendants after you throughout their generations for an everlasting covenant" (Genesis 17:6–7).

This "covenant" marked Israel as unique in all the world. Only Israel could claim to be adopted in this way by the Lord of all the universe. Only Israel could claim to share a bond of kinship with him. Covenants create kinship. They make a family bond. And God had clearly established such a bond with Abraham's descendants.

God promised Israel "kings" as well, and David was the descendant of Abraham who was called to be king over Israel and establish a dynasty that would rule forever. He occupied Israel's throne around 1000 BC. God promised David that his heir would rule not only Israel, but the whole world, and that his reign would be everlasting. "I will make the nations your heritage, and the ends of the earth your possession" (Psalm 2:8). "I will establish the throne of his kingdom for ever" (2 Samuel 7:13).

God makes many promises in the Old Testament, but only twice does he solemnly pledge an oath to bless all nations, once with Abraham and once with David. Significantly, both events took place at the same site, called "Moriah" in the time of Abraham and "Jerusalem" a thousand years later in the time of David (Genesis 22:1–2; 2 Chronicles 3:1).

Those who believed in these ancient promises lived in eager expectation. They had faith that the Son of David would arrive as king over all kings. He would establish peace on the earth, beginning from Israel. Like his ancestor David, he would also be a priest (see Psalm 110:4). David, after all, assumed the right to wear the vestments of the priesthood (1 Samuel 30:7), to offer sacrifice (2 Samuel 6:12–15), and to eat the bread reserved for the clergy of the tribe of Levi (1 Samuel 21:1–6).

For the office of priest-king the Son of David would be anointed, as was his distant ancestor, and he would be known as "the Anointed One"—in Hebrew, *Moshiach*, or Messiah; in Greek, *Christos*; in English, *Christ*.

The promise of a golden age, however, seemed to be dashed to pieces by the sins of David and his heirs, beginning with his son Solomon. David committed adultery and suffered the parricidal wrath of one of his sons. His designated heir, Solomon, taxed his subjects heavily and disobeyed God's commandments, ultimately falling into the gravest of sins: idolatry. Within a generation, David's realm fractured into two rival kingdoms, north and south. Divided and diminished, both the land and the people were left vulnerable to conquest by their neighbors. In the eighth century BC, the Northern Kingdom fell to Assyria. Less than two hundred years later, the south fell to Babylon. Israel's elites were deported; the land was left a ruin; the Temple of God was destroyed; and the line of David was apparently wiped out. Zedekiah, the last Davidic king, was forced to watch while his Chaldean captors executed all his sons. Then they gouged out Zedekiah's eyes, so that his last visual memory would be the corpses of his heirs (see 2 Kings 25:7).

That was the apparent end of the House of David. What, then, were the dispersed and downtrodden people of Israel—God's chosen people—to make of the divine promises?

The prophets sustained their hope. Though all human means seemed to be exhausted, the prophet Isaiah said: "Behold, the LORD's hand is not shortened, that it cannot save" (Isaiah 59:1). God directed his people to watch for the day of the Messiah.

The Messiah would fulfill the role of the *go'el*, the kinsman redeemer; he would be the warrior-hero who would rescue his kin from peril and vindicate their honor. He would arrive within the family. He would arrive as a *son*.

> *For to us a child is born,*
> *to us a son is given;*
> *and the government will be upon his shoulder,*
> *and his name will be called*
> *"Wonderful Counselor, Mighty God,*
> *Everlasting Father, Prince of Peace." (Isaiah 9:6)*

From David's stump would come "a shoot," "a branch" (Isaiah 11:1)—a son—to restore the fortunes squandered by the kings of Israel and Judah. Isaiah foretold what would happen: "Hear then, O house of David! . . . Behold, a virgin shall conceive and bear a son, and shall call his name Immanuel" (Isaiah 7:13–14).

Saint Matthew knew he was tapping into something deep and powerful in his readers. This was *their* story, and they knew it to be an unfinished story—a story in search of an ending. Each of the names in Matthew's catalog evoked a dramatic episode well known to the nation that traced itself back to Abraham. As Matthew moved from one generation to the next, from father to son, we can only imagine the mounting expectation of his first hearers. How would he deal with the extermination of King David's line?

And yet he did! He went on to list fourteen generations "after the deportation to Babylon" (Matthew 1:12)—arriving then at the generation of Jesus.

His entire genealogy is centered on King David and structured in three sets of fourteen generations: "So all the generations from Abraham to David were fourteen generations, and from David to the deportation to Babylon fourteen generations, and from the deportation to Babylon to the

Christ fourteen generations" (Matthew 1:17). Even the number fourteen is a Davidic hallmark. In Hebrew script, numbers are rendered with letters of the alphabet, and the number for fourteen spells out the name David. Matthew has designed his entire opening section to herald Jesus's royal identity.

In beginning his narrative with a genealogy, Saint Matthew was sending a clear message to his kin, to the beleaguered remnant of Abraham's children, who were suffering as their Promised Land was ruled by pagan overlords. The time of the Messiah had arrived. Now would begin the everlasting reign of the true Son of David.

A genealogy is a family record. Traditionally, in patrilineal societies like Israel's, it traced the connections between fathers and sons. In such societies, all history—and society itself—was based on family. Even the bond between kings and their subjects was seen as a "bone and flesh" family bond (see 2 Samuel 5:1). In Israel the connection was more than a metaphor; it was genetically true, as the whole nation claimed descent from Abraham.

Through the prophets God had promised a "son of David . . . son of Abraham," and Matthew made clear at the outset that the promise was now fulfilled in Jesus.

Nevertheless, he punctuated his genealogy with

curiosities—unusual twists and turns that were likely designed to be provocative. He includes women, for example, Tamar, Rahab, Ruth, and Bathsheba (the wife of Uriah). This was rare but not unheard of in the annals of Israel. Some Old Testament genealogies include matriarchal heroes. What is shocking in Matthew's genealogy is the particular women he chose. All four are Gentiles—foreigners, non-Jews—and three of them are associated with sexual immorality. Tamar, a Canaanite, had sexual relations with her father-in-law (Genesis 38:13–18). Rahab, also a Canaanite, was a prostitute by trade (see Joshua 2:1–24). Ruth came from Moab, a people given to idolatry (Ruth 1:4, 15). The most significant woman on the list is Bathsheba, the Hittite woman who committed adultery with King David. Matthew seems to add fuel to the controversial fire by not even listing her by name, but rather as "the wife of Uriah" (Matthew 1:6)—thus drawing attention to her sin of adultery!

What is Matthew doing here? He seems to be making a preemptive apologetic strike. By placing pagan women of ill repute among Jesus's ancestors, Matthew anticipates the arguments of those who would question Jesus's messianic credentials. He goes on to show that Jesus's checkered ancestry, far from undermining his mission, actually confirms it.

Already in the first century the claim of Jesus's virginal conception must have evoked wry smiles from skeptics. This may be the reason that in Saint Mark's Gospel, Jesus's incredulous neighbors call him the "son of Mary" (Mark 6:3). It was customary to refer to a man as the son of his father— unless one wanted to call that fatherhood into question.

Mary's out-of-wedlock pregnancy was a common target in the earliest anti-Christian writings in antiquity. In the Talmud of the Jews, as in the writings of the Greek pagan Celsus, she stands accused of fornication and adultery.[1] Matthew is neutralizing such opposition by showing that conception apart from wedlock does not invalidate Jesus's credentials as Messiah. If it did, then Solomon, the primordial son of David, would be brought down by the same argument.

The ethnicity of these four ancestors is at least as important as their gender. Because it includes Gentiles, Jesus's lineage anticipates the international scope of the Gospel, which extends to "all nations" (see Matthew 28:19). The Messiah's true family—as Jesus himself would reveal—is not tribal, ethnic, or national. It is "born, not of blood nor of the will of the flesh nor of the will of man, but of God" (John 1:13). After asking, "Who is my mother, and who are my brothers?" he answers: "Whoever does the will of my Father in heaven is my brother, and sister, and mother" (Matthew 12:48–50).

In the opening lines of the first Gospel, Matthew prepares the way for a radical rethinking of family relations. The King, the Messiah, the Savior arrived as a son—as expected—but, in doing so he revolutionized our very ideas of sonship and fatherhood and motherhood and family.

And it was not a merely academic discussion. The question of Jesus's identity—and thus his ancestry—demanded a "yes" or a "no." The dilemma created fault lines throughout the clans in Palestine, and in every home where Jews were becoming Christian. Everyone could agree that Solomon was a true son of David, in spite of his imperfect ancestry. Could the same be true of Jesus?

Critical readers will sometimes point out "discrepancies" between the genealogy in Matthew's Gospel and its counterpart in Luke. There are indeed differences between the two. I've already mentioned one. Matthew *launched* his Gospel with Jesus's genealogy; it's the immediate prelude to the account of Jesus's conception and birth. Luke presents the ancestry much later in his narrative, at the beginning of Jesus's public life.

Another discrepancy is the relative size of the lists. Luke's is larger by far, counting seventy-seven generations to Matthew's forty-two.

The evangelists diverge also in their methods. Matthew traces Jesus's lineage forward from Abraham, while Luke traces it backward from Jesus. Luke, moreover, does not stop when he reaches Abraham, but keeps tracing the generations backward till he reaches Adam, the first man. Luke's purpose is clear. While Matthew wants to establish Jesus's credentials as the Messiah of Israel, Luke wants the Gentiles to see him also as Savior of the world.

In following the trail all the way to Adam, moreover, Luke is evoking what Christians would call the Protoevangelion, or "First Gospel," the famous passage of Genesis (3:15) in which God mysteriously foretells "enmity" between Satan and the "seed" of the woman. The Genesis passage is unique in speaking of a particular child as a *woman's* "seed"; the term normally applies to the son's relationship with his father. Christians traditionally have seen this as referring to Jesus, who had no biological father. In all of history, only he could truly be called the "seed" of a woman. By harking back to this most ancient oracle, Luke is, once again, showing that the longing for a deliverer belongs not only to Israel, but to all humanity.

The greatest divergences between Matthew and Luke appear in the evangelists' accounts of the generations between David and Jesus. The two genealogies actually correspond closely until that point; afterward, however, they are almost entirely different. The divergence begins immediately after David. Matthew traces Jesus's lineage through Solomon, who was David's heir as king. Luke shows descent from one of David's older sons, Nathan. After that, the genealogies share only two names in common: Shealtiel and Zerubbabel.

Even the earliest Christians puzzled over the different

approaches of Matthew and Luke, and the early Church Fathers were among the first commentators to propose possible resolutions. At the beginning of the fourth century, the scholarly bishop Eusebius began his book *On the Discrepancies of the Gospels* with an extended discussion of the genealogies, and he drew much of his material from the widely traveled historian Sextus Julius Africanus, who had lived a hundred years before.[2]

Many saints and scholars hold that Luke is tracing Jesus's genealogy through his mother, Mary, while Matthew traces it through his adoptive father, Joseph. This is plausible, since it corresponds to the perspective the evangelists maintain all through their infancy narratives. Matthew consistently presents Joseph's point of view—his intentions, his dreams, and so on. Luke consistently tells Mary's story, from the moment of the annunciation forward. Even before we read the story of the annunciation, Mary's kin, Zechariah and Elizabeth, are the first people we meet in Luke's Gospel.

Others point out that Matthew's genealogy emphasizes Jesus's *kingly* heritage, while Luke's focuses on his priestly ancestors. Again, this corresponds to the rest of their Gospels as well. In Matthew, Jesus is hailed often as "Son of David." Luke's Gospel opens in the precincts of the Temple amid a drama in a priestly family; the motifs of sacrifice recur often in his telling of Jesus's life. (So much so, in fact, that Luke is often portrayed symbolically in Catholic art as an ox, because the ox was a common sacrificial victim.)

These two approaches are not contradictory, and they may be complementary.

Historians have found other ways to reconcile discrepancies between Matthew and Luke. Some ancestors may have borne more than one name (Solomon, for example, was also called Jedidiah; see 2 Samuel 12:24–25), so they may be listed differently in different places. Others may have had two fathers, one by birth and one by adoption, so they may be listed differently in different accounts.

It would be easy to fill a book with all the many hypotheses and speculative solutions inspired by the differences between the New Testament's dueling genealogies. The material is fascinating for a certain sort of scholar, and I confess that I am that sort. But I know that most people are not.

Too often we want the evangelists to behave the way professionals in their field would behave in the modern era. If they're writing history, we want them to supply sources for every claim they make, and we want to be able to check those sources. If they're writing genealogy, we want it to be presented in a form that corresponds with the book that a friend of mine got for his family. It gave an exhaustive account of every generation since his first ancestor arrived on American shores in the seventeenth century. That covers just four hundred years, and the book is almost as hefty as my office dictionary. Imagine what Matthew and Luke would have to provide to cover the thousands of years from the patriarchs to Jesus!

But that's not what the evangelists wanted to do with their genealogies. They wanted not to give a strict accounting, but rather to present the shape of the historical progression. Matthew does this in three symmetrical movements, first patriarchs, then kings, then common citizens. Thus, the very trajectory of the generations shows how God descended to be one with lowliest humanity. What better way to introduce the King Messiah's birth in a stable? Though both Matthew and Luke gave us a true accounting of Jesus's family of origin, neither evangelist was striving for completeness.

Both, however, succeeded in establishing Jesus's identity, and they did so by establishing his family relations. He is King and Messiah. He is High Priest and Redeemer of Israel. He is the agent of a new creation. He is all this because he is, first of all, the Son.

CHAPTER

4

THE COUNTERFEIT KINGDOM

*W*HEN *MARTIN LUTHER KING JR.* delivered his famous "I Have a Dream" speech in 1963, he didn't
make an argument; he delivered a message, and he delivered
it in the most powerful terms. Without stopping to cite his
sources, he invoked popular hymns and spirituals, the biblical prophets Amos and Isaiah, the American Declaration
of Independence, the United States Constitution, and Abraham Lincoln's Emancipation Proclamation. He quoted and
he paraphrased. Sometimes he dropped only a word or name
or image. None required explanation or backstory. Dr. King
was borrowing emotional power from many shared cultural
resources—the stuff that everybody just *knew*.[1]

Matthew depended on similar cultural references as he
composed his first chapter. The history of Israel, the oracles
of the prophets, the expectation of a Messiah, the conditions

of the Messiah's coming—these were details that people in first-century Palestine just *knew*.

The New Testament conveys this ripe sense of expectation. The Jews of Jesus's time believed that the Messiah's arrival was imminent—any day now—not far off. Not only do we see this in the way the crowds followed Jesus. We also learn this because they looked to other messianic claimants. In the Acts of the Apostles, the great rabbi Gamaliel mentions two:

> For before these days Theudas arose, giving himself out to be somebody, and a number of men, about four hundred, joined him; but he was slain and all who followed him were dispersed and came to nothing. After him Judas the Galilean arose in the days of the census and drew away some of the people after him; he also perished, and all who followed him were scattered. (Acts 5:36–37)

Other first-century Jewish authors name other would-be messiahs. The historian Flavius Josephus mentions more than a dozen who lived in or near the time of Jesus. That's a remarkable number of saviors to appear in a land the size of New Jersey, whose population was probably just a fraction of New Jersey's today.

The expectation was palpable. It pervades the documents

that have survived from that period. For the community that preserved the Dead Sea Scrolls, it was practically an obsession. They made minute plans for ritual worship in the time of the Messiah. They sketched out strategies for the battles in which he would lead them to reconquer the lands that were the traditional patrimony of Israel—the entirety of the Promised Land.

The expectation of the Messiah appears also in the ancient Targums.[2] These are expansive "translations" of many of the books of the Hebrew Bible. They're more like paraphrases, and much of the added material concerns the Messiah—how he would come from the tribe of Judah and the line of King David, how he would overthrow the pagans who oppressed Israel, how he would re-establish the Temple and exercise judgment over everyone, sending wicked people to hell (Gehenna) and the good to paradise.

The Targums reflect the expectation of the times—and the Targums themselves surely reinforced that expectation. The Targums were probably read aloud in the synagogue liturgies on the Sabbath and holy days. They fueled the prayer of Israel's families.

Expectation of the Messiah was especially intense in the first centuries before Christ. People believed the time of fulfillment was at hand. And they could point to seemingly good reasons for their hope.

The Hasmonean dynasty ruled Judea from 140 BC till 37 BC. Under John Hyrcanus, the Jewish kingdom conquered the land of Idumea (biblical Edom), to the south, near the Dead Sea. John Hyrcanus required all the Edomites to keep Jewish law or go into exile. This meant strict dietary regulations for everyone and circumcision for all males. Most of the Edomites accepted the terms and stayed—though they were never quite accepted as "real Jews" by the Pharisees or other religious elites.

Still, they managed to grow in influence, especially by negotiating alliances with Rome, then just emerging as a world power.

From among the Edomites arose a man who seemed eager and able to restore the fortunes of Israel in the very terms of God's covenant with David. His name was Herod. Historians refer to him as Herod the Great.

Named "King of the Jews" around 40 BC, Herod completed the conquests begun by the Hasmoneans, taking almost all the lands that had belonged to Israel at the time of the Davidic monarchy. He tried mightily to make himself look like the "son of David." As Solomon had built the first Temple, so Herod rebuilt the second Temple, this time on an epic scale.

He was a shrewd strategist. At first a close ally of Marc Antony and Cleopatra, Herod managed to shift his allegiance to their rival, Octavian (Augustus), just as Octavian was poised for victory. And the Jewish people prospered. Herod founded new cities and initiated extravagant building projects. With the military backing of his Roman patrons, he brought some measure of peace, stability, and security to the region.

Herod made a show of his religious observance. He was scrupulous about observing the Jewish dietary laws. And his Temple reconstruction, though only begun, was clearly intended to be spectacular. He allowed only priests, whose hands had been consecrated for sacred purposes, to work on its construction.

Even so, in the eyes of the elites, he remained a Gentile, an Edomite—and, therefore, he could never be more than an ersatz monarch for the Jews. He knew that they had tolerated him because they prospered from his reign. He tried to manipulate public opinion by removing the Jerusalem high priest and giving the job to his father-in-law, but that only made matters worse.

His insecurities consumed him and led to monstrous suspicions. Though his accomplishments earned him the title "Great," he was, by all contemporary accounts, quite insane. He arranged the murder of his wife Mariamne and three of his sons—Alexander, Aristobulus, and Antipater—because he feared they would plot his overthrow. His paranoid spells often ended in murderous purges of his subjects, too. Once he had hundreds of suspected conspirators crucified along a busy highway, and he left their bodies there to rot on their crosses for weeks.

Because Herod was outwardly pious and sadistically cruel, his behavior moved Caesar Augustus to remark: "It's better to be Herod's pig than his son."[3] A pig, presumably, would be safe from a king who keeps kosher.

Nevertheless, Herod was a genius of sorts—a despicable genius. His successes were impressive: the reconstitution of the Promised Land, the recovery of the tribes that had mingled with the pagans, and the reconstruction of the Temple. In his successes, so many of the prophecies appeared to be fulfilled, and the conditions for the Messiah seemed to be in place.

Speculation indeed was rife in Jerusalem. According to one historical account, the Temple priests had concluded, based on their study of the prophet Daniel, that the time of the Messiah had arrived. The seventy weeks of years (see Daniel 9) had run its course, they said. In the course of their investigation they reviewed every possible candidate and early on eliminated Herod as a possibility. "The priests mourned and grieved to one another in secret for they did not dare to do so openly out of fear of Herod and his friends. They said, 'Our Law bids us to have no foreigner for king.' "[4] The king, of course, caught wind of their judgment and ordered their execution.

Some people, too, wondered whether Herod might indeed be the Son of David. After all, even Solomon had shortcomings. If the original son of David was guilty of idolatry, polygamy, oppressive taxation, and profound disobedience of God, couldn't the new son of David be forgiven a murderous spree every now and then?

There was a still more dangerous corollary to the first century's messianic speculation. If Herod was *not* the Anointed One, could he be, perhaps, a forerunner—someone sent by God simply to prepare the way and then get out of the way?

It's quite possible that Herod suspected this—and expected a true "son of David" to arrive at any moment. And where would that leave the current king?

It seems there was an intense and uneasy awareness, shared by everyone from the kings to the priests, that the time of the Messiah was at hand.

The expectation even touched the pagan world. The Roman poet Virgil saw in the rise of Caesar Augustus the fulfillment of the hopes and fears of all the years. In his fourth Eclogue he addresses a prayer to the goddess of childbirth to bless the future emperor as he was born.

Smile at the birth of the boy, chaste Lucina.
In him the iron age shall cease and the golden age arise. . . .
This glorious age shall begin,
and the months enter on their mighty march.

Then Virgil says to Augustus:

Under your guidance, whatever tracks remain
of our old wickedness, once done away,
shall free the earth from never-ceasing fear.

He concludes:

He shall receive the life of gods, and he shall . . .
with his father's worth reign over a world at peace.[5]

It was almost as if the whole world sensed, but dimly, that it was reaching a climactic moment in history. It was almost as if people were already seeking an explanation for an event that was inevitable.

Even angelic intelligences must have sensed that something was happening. And if the fallen angels detected God's imminent intervention, they certainly would have thrown up distractions in key places—feigned the fulfillment of prophecies by conspicuous figures, such as kings and emperors.

Meanwhile, late in the reign of King Herod, in a sleepy corner of Israel's lands, the Messiah arrived.

One of the earliest Christian authors whose writings have survived, Saint Ignatius of Antioch, tells us that the coming of the Christ, "wrought in silence," was "hidden from the prince of this world."[6]

It would not be hidden for long from Herod.

CHAPTER

5

MARY: CAUSE OF OUR JOY

*S*HE HAS INSPIRED MANY of the greatest works of poetry, music, painting, sculpture, and monumental architecture. Hers is the expressive power that animates the *Pietà* of Michelangelo. To her honor, the architects of the Middle Ages raised the great cathedrals of Chartres and Notre Dame. The Sistine Chapel was dedicated to her memory. Countless voices call her name to the melodies of Schubert's or Bach's "Ave Maria." She and her divine child are at the center of Raphael's great *Sistine Madonna;* and she is the subject of masterworks by artists from Giotto, Duccio, Cimabue, and Leonardo da Vinci down to Picasso and Salvador Dalí.

The Church invokes her under dozens of titles, some poetic and some theologically technical. She is the Blessed Virgin, Mother of God, Queen of Angels, Immaculate

Conception, Refuge of Sinners, Comforter of the Afflicted, Mystical Rose. . . .

All those names and cultural artifacts have formed us as Christians, and they have formed our impressions of her. They are like the gold that the early Christians sometimes used to encase the relics of the cross. They're beautiful and fitting, but they can also have the unintended effect of obscuring what they were fashioned to honor. The cross that bore our salvation was made from common wood.

Similarly, the Ark of the New Covenant—the vessel of honor—the young woman who bore our salvation from the moment of his descent from heaven was, in many respects, an ordinary girl from a no-account place.

If we want to know the Blessed Virgin as she truly is, we must come to see her as she was—before anyone knew the magnitude of her glory—as she grew to maturity in the dusty village of Nazareth.

Nazareth is today the largest city in the northern district of Israel. Its population falls just shy of a quarter of a million people. In the first century before Christ, however, it likely had no more than a few hundred inhabitants, most of them living in stone caves cut into the hillside. Nazareth surely enjoyed some economic benefit from Herod's nearby building projects, but still the village made hardly any impression on outsiders. Nathanael's remark to Philip, at the beginning of Saint John's Gospel, was probably a typical city dweller's reaction to a backwater village: "Can anything good come out of Nazareth?" (John 1:46).

The root of *Nazareth* seems to be the Hebrew word *nezer*, which means "branch." We don't know how the village got its name. But Christians saw in Nazareth a fulfillment of one of the prophet Isaiah's oracles about the Messiah: "There shall come forth a shoot from the stump of Jesse, and a *branch* shall grow out of his roots" (Isaiah 11:1). Since Jesse was the father of King David, the "stump" clearly symbolized his family tree, which had been reduced almost to nothing. Out of the stump would come a "branch"—the Son of David who, according to the verses that followed, would be filled with the Holy Spirit and would inaugurate an age of peace, not only for Israel, but for the Gentiles, too. "In that day," Isaiah foretold, "the root of Jesse shall stand as an ensign to the peoples; him shall the nations seek, and his dwellings shall be glorious" (Isaiah 11:10).

Today the centerpiece of Nazareth is the Basilica of the Annunciation, built over the "venerated grotto"—the remains of the humble cave that served as the childhood home of Mary, the Mother of Jesus. The church's altar is inscribed with the Latin words *Verbum caro hic factum est*—"Here the Word became flesh!"

It was *there,* in a well-swept, well-kept cave, that "the angel of the Lord declared unto Mary, and she conceived by the Holy Spirit."

We know little with certainty about Mary's childhood—only what we can surmise from a careful reading of her words recorded in the Gospels. From her words it's clear that she grew up in a pious household. She knew the Scriptures of Israel, the books we know as the Old Testament, and she could quote them and allude to them with ease. It is unlikely that she owned any books; she would have known the Bible mostly from its proclamation in the local synagogue, and from dinnertime discussions at home and with her friends. She had well-developed habits of prayer, and she did not stumble or hesitate as she conversed with an archangel.

In artwork she is often shown at work, and that is surely an accurate depiction. Home life in those days was labor-intensive. There were no appliances to take care of common tasks—cooking, cleaning, laundry—and these required dedicated attention.

When we meet her in the Gospels, she is already "betrothed" to a man. So she was probably in her early teens, perhaps as young as thirteen. Life expectancy was around thirty for men and less for women. Girls usually entered arranged marriages shortly after puberty and menarche. The men they married were usually at least a few years older, having proven themselves capable of supporting a family.

❈

We know, too, that Mary enjoyed a close family bond with Zechariah and Elizabeth, who were her kin. We don't know the degree of their relationship. They may have been Mary's cousins, or even her aunt and uncle. Her bond with them was intimate despite the fact that they lived almost ninety miles away, to the south of Nazareth, in the village of Ein Karem. When Mary heard that Elizabeth was pregnant, she wanted to help her kinswoman, so she made the arduous journey "with haste" (Luke 1:39).

There are many possible explanations for the closeness of Mary and Elizabeth. If the older couple had always lived in Ein Karem, Mary may have known them from her family's thrice-yearly holy-day pilgrimages to nearby Jerusalem (for the feasts of Passover, Weeks, and Booths). It could be, too, that Zechariah and Elizabeth had once lived in Nazareth and only late in life moved to Ein Karem to be closer to Jerusalem for Zechariah's priestly service.

As a priest, Zechariah held a hereditary office reserved to men from the tribe of Levi. Only the Levitical priests could perform the rites and offer sacrifice in the Temple. The Levites had no territory of their own. Instead they were dispersed through the lands of the other tribes. Adult males began their priestly service later in life, organized into one of twenty-four "divisions," and their terms of service rotated through the year. Many priestly families, like Zechariah's, chose to live near Jerusalem for the sake of their ministry.

An ancient tradition holds that Mary herself served a role in the Temple; and if that is true, she could have stayed at the home of her relatives during her term of service.

What could such a role have been? The *Protoevangelium of James*, probably composed around AD 125, says that from the age of three through twelve, "Mary was in the temple of the Lord as if she were a dove that dwelt there, and she received food from the hand of an angel." The text describes Mary performing menial tasks, such as fetching water, but also skilled craftwork. She is chosen from among Israel's consecrated virgins to weave the intricate veil for the Temple's holy of holies.[1]

Though the *Protoevangelium* was composed late, compared to the Gospels, it is still one of the earliest Christian documents that have survived to our day. It has neither the authority nor the understated quality of the canonical Gospels. It does, however, tell us much about what Christians believed about the Blessed Virgin not long after she ended her earthly days (and the traditions they preserved). And many of the details are not as far-fetched as the *Protoevangelium*'s breathless style might suggest.

The Torah speaks, after all, of "ministering women who ministered at the door of the tent of meeting," the precursor to Israel's Temple (see Exodus 38:8). The same office appears centuries later, during the time of Eli (see 1 Samuel 2:22). The Second Book of Maccabees, written in the second century BC, confirms another detail of the account, as it speaks of consecrated virgins who are cloistered within the Temple and who dedicate themselves to prayer (2 Maccabees 3:19–20). Similarly, the *Apocalypse of Baruch*, probably composed in Hebrew in the first century AD, speaks of the Temple's "virgins who weave fine linen and silk with gold of Ophir."[2]

We know that Mary had family connections to the Jerusalem priesthood. We know, furthermore—from several sources—that young women offered dedicated service of prayer at the Temple. Our sources attest to this custom in the times of Moses, David, and Jesus.

We can, therefore, at least acknowledge the *possibility* that Mary spent part of her childhood in service at the Temple, as the apocryphal accounts claim she did, and that she was consecrated for this purpose.

In any event, we can be sure that Mary, having lived in the home of the priest Zechariah, was familiar with many of the customs of priestly service; the traditions of the Jerusalem Temple must have influenced her piety, and in turn the piety of the household she kept as a wife and mother.

The most controversial aspect of Temple service—and the most controversial aspect of Mary's special role in the Messiah's story—is virginity. As we mentioned in our chapter on Jesus's genealogy, non-Christians called Mary's chastity and honor into question as early as the first and second centuries. The *Protoevangelium of James* thought it helpful to invoke the testimony of a midwife on Mary's behalf.

The fact of Mary's virginity was clearly important to the first Christians. Saint Matthew's Gospel sets it forth as the fulfillment of Isaiah's prophecy of the Messiah: "All this took place to fulfill what the Lord had spoken by the prophet: 'Behold, a virgin shall conceive and bear a son, and his name shall be called Emmanuel' (which means, God with us)" (Matthew 1:22–23, quoting Isaiah 7:14).

Matthew quotes the oracle as it is found in the Septuagint, the most ancient translation of the Old Testament into Greek, which was completed in the third or second century BC. Why is this important? Because the Septuagint renders the Hebrew word *almah* with the Greek word *parthenos*—virgin—whereas later (post-Christian) Jewish translations render it as "young woman." This led Saint Justin Martyr and Saint Irenaeus of Lyons, both writing in the middle of the second century AD, to accuse the Jews of their time of changing Scripture to accommodate their anti-Christian polemics.[3]

Now, *almah* can be rendered as either "virgin" or "young woman." The terminology in other languages is similarly ambiguous—the German *jungfrau,* for example. But what did Isaiah intend? And what did the Jews of the first century BC understand by the oracle?

We cannot read Isaiah's mind, but we can read his context. The passage opens with the challenge: "Ask a sign of the LORD your God; let it be deep as Sheol or high as heaven" (Isaiah 7:11). He seems to be talking about a momentous sign, something indisputably miraculous. A virgin bearing a son would indeed be such a singular event. A "young woman" bearing a son would be unremarkable and underwhelming, as signs go.

Thus we can probably trust the authority of the Septuagint—which enjoyed a semi-official status in the Jewish diaspora and was uninfluenced by later Christian-Jewish disputes.

Mary's virginal motherhood is a sign. It is not, however, a statement against the goodness of sex, as some heretics later claimed it was. It is rather a guarantee of God's fatherhood— God is the only *possible* father of Jesus—and at the same time it is recognition of Mary's special status as the mother of the Messiah. She was, as such, a vessel of the divine. Her body was, in a sense, like the golden vessels dedicated for Temple service. It was forbidden to use such chalices and plates at even the most dignified royal banquet. Likewise, her womb, having borne the Savior, could not return to ordinary activity, no matter how good, no matter how blessed.

Her perpetual virginity was fitting and proper to her unique role in the history of salvation. It is interesting to note that for the early Christians she was "the Virgin"—as if she had a special claim on the noun and required the definite article. It is the same grammatical construction found in the earliest Hebrew manuscripts of Isaiah 7:14.

But was Mary's virginity chosen? Had she already committed her life to God before the angel visited her?

Mary's dialogue with the angel is indeed curious.

In the sixth month the angel Gabriel was sent from God to a city of Galilee named Nazareth, to a virgin betrothed to a man whose name was Joseph, of the house of David; and the virgin's name was Mary. And he came to her and said, "Hail, full of grace, the Lord is with you!" But she was greatly troubled at the saying, and considered in her mind what sort of greeting this might be. And the angel said to her, "Do not be afraid, Mary, for you have found favor with God. And behold, you will conceive in your womb and bear a son, and you shall call his name Jesus.

"He will be great, and will be called the Son of the Most High; and the Lord God will give to him the throne of his father David, and he will reign over the house of Jacob for ever; and of his kingdom there will be no end."

And Mary said to the angel, "How shall this be, since I have no husband?" And the angel said to her,

"The Holy Spirit will come upon you, and the power of the Most High will overshadow you; therefore the child to be born will be called holy, the Son of God." (Luke 1:26–35)

A more literal rendering of Mary's question would be: "How shall this be, since I do not know man?" "To know" is the common Hebrew idiom for sexual union. In the book of Genesis we read: "Cain knew his wife, and she conceived and bore Enoch. . . . Adam knew his wife again, and she bore a son and called his name Seth" (Genesis 4:17, 25). Still today we use the phrase "carnal knowledge" as a kind of polite phrase for sexual intercourse.

The connection between "knowing" and "conception" was clear in the Torah as it was in life. So what could Mary have meant by her question? The angel had told her she would conceive a son, and she did not understand how that could be. She had not carried out what she knew to be the requisite act for pregnancy.

It's not that Mary was ignorant of the facts of life. She genuinely wanted to know how the angel Gabriel's announcement could be true. Reading this passage, Saint Augustine noted: "Surely she would not have said this unless she had already vowed herself to God as a virgin. . . . Certainly she would not have asked, how, being a female, she should give birth to her promised son, if she had married with the purpose of sexual intercourse."[4]

According to Christian tradition, Mary remained perpetually a virgin—before Jesus's birth and after. Even before his conception, she may have discerned a special call to consecrated virginity. We have already seen that such commitments, though rare in Judaism, had ample precedent. Allow me to explain.

Celibacy may have been more common than modern scholars—and Christianity's ancient opponents, too—have been willing to acknowledge. Let's consider the sources.

First-century Judaism is an obscure and enigmatic subject of study. Our primary sources for knowledge of the period are the writings of Philo of Alexandria, a Jewish philosopher living in Egypt; the histories of Josephus (whom we've already encountered); the Dead Sea Scrolls, which were produced by a Jewish sect, or sects; and the documents of the New Testament.

Philo gives at least two examples of Jews observing celibacy. In his *Apology for the Jews,* he tells of a sect called the

Essenes: "They banned marriage at the same time as they ordered the practice of perfect continence."[5] The Essenes seem, from all accounts, to have lived in Palestine, concentrating especially in the desert area near the Dead Sea. In his treatise *The Contemplative Life*, Philo describes another Jewish sect, called the Therapeutae. Perhaps related to the Essenes, the Therapeutae flourished in Egypt, and they also seem to have practiced celibacy and continence.

The historian Josephus discussed the Essenes at greater length and recorded that "they disdain marriage for themselves"[6] and "they take no wives."[7]

Even Gentiles took notice of Essene celibacy. The Roman naturalist Pliny the Elder, writing in the first century, quipped that the desert dwellers lived without mates, "renouncing love altogether . . . having only the date palms for company."[8]

It is worth noting that several well-known Jewish figures of the first century observed celibacy: John the Baptist, Jesus, and Saint Paul. No one seems to have thought John odd for his renunciation of marriage—only for his diet of locusts and his clothing of camel hair. It is interesting, too, that Saint Paul devoted part of his First Letter to the Corinthians (chapter 7) to the subject of consecrated virginity and celibacy, and he assumed that there were already many people living that lifestyle in the Church. Jesus, who was celibate himself, did not treat celibacy as his own idiosyncrasy or prerogative but rather assumed that others would follow the same path (see, for example, Matthew 19:10–12).

Mary's virginal, divine motherhood was certainly a miraculous and unique event. But her virginity itself is not the far-fetched notion that some critics make it out to be. The tradition of consecrated virginity likely predated Christianity, though with Christianity it became commonplace. Wherever there were Christian churches, there were many women dedicated to perpetual virginity. The evidence is abundant from the first generation—the time of the Apostolic Fathers— onward. In every church, these consecrated women took as their model the poor girl from Nazareth.

Fundamentalist Protestants sometimes complain that Catholics exaggerate the role of the Blessed Virgin. But it is history itself—salvation history—that has given her an outsized role. It is the Lord of history who cast her for such a part in the drama.

Her lines in Saint Luke's Gospel add up to far more than a cameo appearance. The story of redemption turns on her brief dialogue with the angel. Heaven awaits her response. The Church has ever since echoed her prayer, the *Magnificat*.

My soul magnifies the Lord,

and my spirit rejoices in God my Savior,

for he has regarded the low estate of his handmaiden.

For behold, henceforth all generations will call me blessed;

for he who is mighty has done great things for me,

and holy is his name.

And his mercy is on those who fear him

from generation to generation.

He has shown strength with his arm,

he has scattered the proud in the imagination of their hearts,

he has put down the mighty from their thrones,

and exalted those of low degree;

he has filled the hungry with good things,

and the rich he has sent empty away.

He has helped his servant Israel,

in remembrance of his mercy,

as he spoke to our fathers,

to Abraham and to his posterity for ever. (Luke 1:46–55)

Mary of Nazareth gave the Church—and every Christian—the model prayer of praise and thanksgiving. It is a model prayer for Christmas. She taught the world the proper response to God who has made his dwelling among humankind—who has made his dwelling in her flesh and in ours.

Saint Luke presents the Virgin of Nazareth as an icon of human freedom and human dignity. There is nothing obsequious about her. She is "troubled" by the angel's presence, but she still dares to inquire. Hers is an active and intelligent obedience.

Tradition honors Mary as the "Virgin of Tenderness," and she is tender. Yet the lines of the *Magnificat* also show us a fierceness of fidelity. It is a quality God cultivated in Israel, a quality that enabled a faithful remnant to keep faith in spite of exile and oppression.

All of Mary's qualities are graces from God. In her we see grace in an extraordinary degree because of the way God prepared her for her unique vocation.

But Catholic theology insists that grace builds upon nature. The God who created us is the same God who redeemed us and calls us. And so it is not at all fanciful for us to see Mary's *Magnificat* as a window into her upbringing. Her ancestor King David was a shepherd of sheep before he became a shepherd of Israel. Mary's fidelity, her knowledge of the history of Israel, her faithfulness to the law of Moses, her reverence for the Temple, her habits of prayer, praise, and gratitude—all of these are a tribute to her family of origin and a childhood spent in the courts of the Lord.

Though her speaking role diminishes after Jesus's childhood, she still looms large in the Gospel. She remains with him, and that seems perfectly in character. The young woman who would dare to question an angel would become the sort of older woman who could spend years following after a son who had "nowhere to lay his head" (Matthew 8:20).

That is the tenderness and the tenacity God created, saw, and loved in Israel, his bride and daughter and firstborn. Those are the characteristics that God gives as a grace and loves in his earthly family, beginning with his mother.

SILENT KNIGHT, HOLY KNIGHT

IN THIRTY YEARS OF active church and academic work, I've taught thousands of classes. I've written several dozen books and countless articles, and I've recorded audio courses and lectures whose distribution numbers in the millions. I've hosted more than a dozen television series and appeared on hundreds of radio shows. I've given thousands of parish and conference talks, in many countries on many continents— and even on the high seas.

I say none of this to brag, but rather to show that all those millions of words I've produced add up to less than an anthill when I compare them to the mountainous accomplishments of one great *silent* man: Joseph of Nazareth.

Christians have always held the man in fascination. The New Testament begins by telling the events of salvation from his point of view. Some of history's greatest minds have pondered his actions—from Augustine through Aquinas to John Paul II. Yet we do not know a single syllable of a single word he ever spoke.

Certainly we can assume he prayed the traditional prayers of Israel—the prayers we find, for example, on the lips of his adopted son, Jesus: "Hear, O Israel: The Lord our God, the Lord is one; and you shall love the Lord your God with all your heart, and with all your soul, and with all your mind, and with all your strength" (Mark 12:29–30). Jesus was truly human and had to learn his prayers from someone—quite likely from his parents. We do know that Jesus was obedient to Joseph and to Mary (Luke 2:51).

Not even the most prolific author in all of history can claim to have had such influence—to have influenced God himself. And yet, as I said, we possess not a word that we can call Saint Joseph's.

What we have are his deeds—and his silence, which is itself significant. One of the bestselling modern biographies of Mary's husband is titled *Joseph the Silent.*[1] No one, I'm afraid, will ever write even a paragraph about me with the title "Scott the Silent."

But Joseph's *actions* speak volumes. Like great poetry, they speak eloquently, if sometimes enigmatically. And almost everything we know about the man we find in the Christmas story.

❀

Joseph the Silent enters history in an uncharacteristic way. Saint Matthew's genealogy moves from one generation to the next by saying that a particular man is "father of" a particular son: "Matthan the father of Jacob, and Jacob the father of Joseph . . ." As the roll draws to its close, however, it identifies Joseph not as a father, but as *"the husband of Mary,* of whom Jesus was born, who is called Christ" (Matthew 1:15–16).

The final link breaks with the preceding pattern. Joseph is not called *father,* but *spouse.* The evangelist wants to be perfectly clear that Joseph had no biological role to play in the conception of Jesus. This important detail prepares readers for the account of the virginal conception of Jesus a couple verses later, in Matthew 1:18–25.

This does not make Joseph any less a father. By Jewish law, he was Jesus's father, and this is evident in Matthew 1:25, when Joseph exercises the father's right to name the child. He exercises all the duties of fatherhood, moreover, by protecting Mary and Jesus and supporting them through the dangers of Herod's reign (see Matthew 2:13–22). According to Jewish custom, Jesus received full hereditary rights through Joseph, even though he was adopted.

Pious Christians will sometimes refer to Joseph as Jesus's

"foster father," so as to build a rhetorical wall around Mary's virginity and God's fatherhood. As a theologian, I value precision, and I respect this usage, but we must be clear about our purposes.

The simple fact is that an adoptive father is as much a father as a natural father is. That was true in Jesus's day as it is in our own; it was recognized in Israel's law and Roman law, and it remains true of the laws of the state in which I live. With my own eyes, I have seen it to be true in countless families. For those reasons and others, I think that the term "foster father," when applied to Saint Joseph, can sometimes hinder as much as it helps.

From the testimony of Scripture, we know that in the Holy Family, Joseph was Jesus's father. That's the word we find in Luke 2:33. When the Virgin Mary speaks to Jesus, she refers to her husband as "your father" (Luke 2:48). The neighbors considered Jesus to be "Joseph's son" (Luke 4:22) and "the carpenter's son" (Matthew 13:55).

Joseph's vocation is to be an earthly image of Jesus's heavenly Father. God is more Father than any man on earth, though he fathers without gender, without a body, without sexual organs or a sexual act, and without a spouse. God's fatherhood is perfect, so we know that fatherhood is not primarily *physical*, but rather *spiritual*. The fatherhood of Joseph is spiritual and real, though virginal, just as the fatherhood of God is spiritual and nonphysical.

Saint Joseph serves, then, as an icon of God the Father, and even Jesus would have thought of him in that way. Jesus was truly human, and he thought as humans think. When we think about trees, for example, our reference point is either our sense of perception or our memory of actual trees. When we meditate on God the Father, we draw from some memory or experience of fatherhood. When Jesus addressed or thought of his heavenly Father, he probably relied on the analogy of his earthly father, Saint Joseph.

Later in life, Jesus said, "Whoever does the will of God is my brother, and sister, and mother" (Mark 3:35). He never assigned his disciples the role of father in his life—not even by analogy. That was the singular privilege of Saint Joseph: to be the earthly father of Jesus.

Like everything we have seen so far in Matthew's Gospel, the details about Joseph's life hark back to Israel's heritage. Matthew shows that Joseph, like Jesus and Mary, was foreshadowed in the history of the patriarchs, prefigured more than a thousand years before.

The New Testament Joseph, the husband of Mary, seems a "reprise" of the Old Testament Joseph—Joseph, the son of Jacob, the young man with the coat of many colors. Christians in every age have noted the parallels in their lives.

First the obvious: both share the name Joseph. Both have fathers named Jacob (see Matthew 1:16 and Genesis 30:19–24). God spoke to both of them through dreams (see Matthew 1:20–21 and 2:13-22 and Genesis 37:5–11). Both men were righteous and chaste (see Matthew 1:19 and Genesis 39:7–18). And both saved their families by bringing them to Egypt (see Matthew 2:13–14 and Genesis 45:16–20).

Pope Leo XIII noted this connection between the two great biblical Josephs, concluding that the more ancient Joseph "by his glory prefigured the greatness of the future guardian of the Holy Family."[2]

Joseph was also a "son of David," as Matthew's genealogy makes clear (Matthew 1:1–16); so Joseph was the bearer of the royal birthright, which he passed on to his son and heir, Jesus.

Joseph embodied his heritage best, however, in his righteousness. The Gospel tells us, up front and with the greatest brevity, that Joseph was "a just man" (Matthew 1:19). From a first-century Jew, that was a supreme compliment. It meant that Joseph's life and his dispositions were conformed to God's law. Joseph respected the commandments of God, and he carried them out faithfully.

Such righteousness is one of the preconditions of the drama in Saint Matthew's narrative. The evangelist specifies that the conflict took place because Joseph was "a just [or righteous] man."

Now the birth of Jesus Christ took place in this way. When his mother Mary had been betrothed to Joseph, before they came together she was found to be with child of the Holy Spirit; and her husband Joseph, being a just man and unwilling to put her to shame, resolved to send her away quietly. (Matthew 1:18–19)

Betrothal in ancient Judaism was not like our modern "engagement." It was a temporary period (up to one year) between the covenant of marriage and the time when the spouses lived together. The couples were *legally married* during this intervening phase, so a betrothal could be terminated only by death or divorce (Deuteronomy 24:1–4).

Mary was pregnant during her betrothal to Joseph. He resolved to divorce her. But why?

Well, Joseph doesn't say, of course—because in the Gospels he doesn't say anything at all. And this silence has been unbearable for many close readers, devoted souls who want to reconcile the great man's righteousness with his intention to divorce the Blessed Virgin. Joseph's plan seems incompatible with his character.

Saints and scholars have proposed a number of explanations, which fall into three categories, or theories. They all seek an answer to the question: *Who did Joseph think was the unworthy partner in the betrothal?*

1. The Suspicion Theory

This view holds that Joseph suspected Mary of adultery when he discovered she was pregnant. The troubling news led him to seek a divorce in accordance with the law of Israel: "When a man takes a wife and marries her, if then she finds no favor in his eyes because he has found some indecency in her, . . . he writes her a bill of divorce and puts it in her hand and sends her out of his house, and she departs out of his house" (Deuteronomy 24:1).

According to this theory, Joseph wished to carry out the divorce secretly in order to avoid subjecting Mary to the rigors of the law, which mandated capital punishment for adulterers.

> If there is a betrothed virgin, and a man meets her in the city and lies with her, then you shall bring them both out to the gate of that city, and you shall stone them to death with stones, the young woman because she did not cry for help though she was in the city, and the man because he violated his neighbor's wife; so you shall purge the evil from the midst of you. (Deuteronomy 22:23–24)

Joseph, then, was a just man inasmuch as he resolved to act in accordance with the law of Moses.

While this is a common interpretation, it has serious weaknesses. Joseph's desire to follow the law for divorce does not square with his willingness to sidestep the law prescribed for adulterers. A truly righteous man would keep God's law completely, not selectively. Think of Saul of Tarsus, a man zealous for the law, who was willing to punish the early Christians by stoning them to death, because of their apparent disobedience of the law. If Paul had been in Joseph's place, Mary might have ended up like Stephen (see Acts 7:58–8:1).

2. *The Perplexity Theory*

Others hold that Joseph found the situation of Mary's pregnancy inexplicable. He could not believe her to be capable of infidelity. Yet neither could he imagine another explanation.

Divorce seemed to be his only option, yet he wished to do this quietly, for he did not believe Mary could be guilty. This theory holds Joseph to be righteous because he wished to live by God's law and yet also judge Mary's situation with the utmost charity.

3. *The Reverence Theory*

This view holds that Joseph, already informed of the divine miracle within Mary, considered himself unworthy to be part of God's work in this unusual situation. He was, according to this theory, like Simon Peter who thought himself unworthy of Jesus's company and said: "Depart from me, for I am a sinful man, O Lord" (Luke 5:8). Or he was like the centurion who said to Jesus: "I am not worthy to have you come under my roof" (Luke 7:6).

Joseph's resolve to separate quietly from Mary is thus viewed as a reverent and discretionary measure to keep secret the mystery within her. Thus, his plan of action is consonant with his character as a just man. His righteousness lines up with his intentions. Joseph's "plan," then, is an expression of his profound humility and his reverence for God and for Mary.

One *apparent* obstacle to this theory is not really an obstacle at all. The expression "to put her to shame," which we find in the English translation, is inexact. The Greek does not carry the same negative connotations. The original suggests simply that Joseph did not want to exhibit Mary in a public way, which again is consonant with his reverence for the mystery.

Read in this light, the angel's counsel to Joseph makes perfect sense.

> But as he considered this, behold, an angel of the Lord appeared to him in a dream, saying, "Joseph, son of David, do not fear to take Mary your wife, for that which is conceived in her is of the Holy Spirit." (Matthew 1:20)

The angel directs Joseph to set aside pious fears and inhibitions that would lead him away from his vocation. God is calling Joseph to be the legal father of the Davidic Messiah.

Of the three possible explanations for Joseph's motives, I find this the most satisfying. And I find good company in Saint Thomas Aquinas, Saint Bernard of Clairvaux, and Saint Josemaría Escrivá, who weighed the evidence and came to the same conclusion.

As already noted, the Gospels make clear that Mary conceived her child by the power of the Holy Spirit (see Matthew 1:18, Luke 1:35). No sexual act was involved. Furthermore, according to Christian tradition, Mary remained *perpetually* a virgin. So the couple, Mary and Joseph, never engaged in ordinary marital relations. They were truly husband and wife, but their relationship was not sexually consummated.

Some ancient authors were so anxious to communicate this fact that they denied Joseph the title of husband. "Joseph was always the betrothed," said one, "but never the husband."[3] Another dared to address Joseph directly: "Even though she is named your wife . . . she is not your wife."[4] These are clearly overstatements, since, as we have seen, the Gospels themselves identify Joseph as "the husband of Mary."

The anxiety arose because of two verses in Matthew's Gospel that appeared to suggest a change in Mary and Joseph's relationship after the birth of Jesus.

> When his mother Mary had been betrothed to Joseph, *before* they came together she was found to be with child of the Holy Spirit. (Matthew 1:18)

> Joseph . . . took his wife, but knew her not *until* she had borne a son. (Matthew 1:24–25)

In the fourth century, a heretic named Helvidius seized on this ambiguity and argued against Mary's perpetual virginity. The conjunctions *before* and *until*, he argued, imply that the conditions before Jesus's birth no longer applied once he was born. In other words, he claimed that in the course of time Mary and Joseph "came together" and Joseph "knew her."

Helvidius further noted that all four Gospels refer to

"brothers" of the Lord (see, for example, Matthew 12:46; Mark 3:31; Luke 8:19; John 2:12). These "brothers," he concluded, must have been younger children of Mary and Joseph.

He was bucking the interpretive tradition when he made his case, and he attracted the opposition of the greatest Scripture scholar of his day, Saint Jerome of Stridon, a man of profound erudition, fluent in the biblical languages.

Jerome refuted Helvidius so decisively that more than a millennium would pass before another interpreter would make the same mistake.

Helvidius insisted that the chronology implied by *before* and *until* required a changed circumstance *afterward*. Jerome demonstrated that the words entail no such requirement, and he multiplied counterexamples that use the same Greek conjunctions.

> By the mouth of the prophet, God says to certain persons, "Even until your old age I am he" (Isaiah 46:4). Will he cease to be God when they have grown old?
>
> And the Savior in the Gospel tells the Apostles, "lo, I am with you always, until the close of the age" (Matthew 28:20). Will the Lord then, after the end of the world has come, forsake his disciples?[5]

Jerome continued at great length, and we can follow him in multiplying Scripture passages that dissolve into absurdity when we apply Helvidius's principle: "Michal the daughter of Saul had no child to the day of her death" (2 Samuel 6:23). And did she have children afterward?

Or how about Saint Paul's instruction to Timothy: "Till I come, attend to the public reading of scripture, to preaching, to teaching" (1 Timothy 4:13). Do you think Paul wanted Timothy to *stop* reading Scripture once the apostle had arrived in town?

What, then, are we to make of Helvidius's other point, about the "brothers" of Jesus? Some of the Church Fathers believed that Joseph was a widower and these were his children from his first marriage. That may be true, but it seems unlikely, since these half-siblings appear nowhere in the accounts of Jesus's infancy and childhood.

It is more likely that the "brothers" mentioned in the Gospels were cousins or distant relations. Ancient Semitic languages made no distinctions among blood relations; all in the tribal family, whether siblings or cousins, were called "brothers" and "sisters." Consider James and Joseph, two of the men who are identified in the Gospels as Jesus's "brothers" (see Matthew 13:55). Elsewhere, however, the same men are identified as sons of *Mary, the wife of Clopas* (see Matthew 27:56; Mark 15:40). John, furthermore, identifies this Mary as a "sister" of the Blessed Virgin Mary (see John 19:25). It is unlikely that two women named Mary would be siblings, so they, too, were probably cousins or more distant kin.

The earliest interpreters of Scripture were well aware of the Lord's "brothers," as they were aware of the range of meanings for the prepositions *before* and *until*. They did not see these as threats to the Church's interpretive tradition.

Even the Protestant Reformers John Calvin and Ulrich Zwingli accepted the tradition intact and taught that Joseph and Mary had no sexual relations at any time during their marriage.

Nevertheless, Joseph was truly a husband to Mary—and, more important, truly a father to Jesus. In fact, he is the man who enjoyed fatherhood to a pre-eminent degree. Pope Benedict XVI put it beautifully.

> There is but one fatherhood, that of God the Father, the one Creator of the world, "of all that is seen and unseen." Yet man, created in the image of God, has been granted a share in this one paternity of God (cf. Ephesians 3:15). Saint Joseph is a striking case of this, since he is a father, without fatherhood according to the flesh. He is not the biological father of Jesus, whose Father is God alone, and yet he lives his fatherhood fully and completely. To be a father means above all to be at the service of life and growth. Saint Joseph, in this sense, gave proof of great

devotion. For the sake of Christ he experienced persecution, exile and the poverty which this entails. He had to settle far from his native town. His only reward was to be with Christ.[6]

It is the only reward any Christian, father or mother, should hope for.

ANGELS: ECHOING THEIR JOYOUS STRAINS

*C*HRISTMAS WOULD BE INCONCEIVABLE without angels.[1] From the moment of Jesus's conception, these pure spirits played crucial parts in the drama. They reappear at almost every milestone in the infancy of Jesus—from Nazareth to Bethlehem, from Jerusalem to Egypt.

That's the reason so many people keep an angel atop their Christmas tree or manger set. It completes the scene. Those who don't have an angel usually have a Bethlehem star—which, according to some of the Church Fathers, was an angel anyway. (More on that in a later chapter.)

Every story has a backstory, and, as we've seen, the human backstory of Christmas reaches back to the beginning of time. Jesus's genealogy leads us to Adam. The promise of a Messiah echoes through history because God himself made the promise as he expelled Adam and Eve from the Garden of Eden.

What most people don't know is that the backstory begins even earlier for the angels. The event that brought joy to our world—the incarnation of God—brought joy to the angelic world as well.

When the early Christians read the story of Christmas, it took them back not only to the story of Adam and Eve, but to the very first lines of the Bible:

> In the beginning God created the heavens and the earth. . . . And God said, "Let there be light"; and there was light. And God saw that the light was good; and God separated the light from the darkness. (Genesis 1:1, 3–4)

Saint Augustine and Saint Ambrose insisted that the "heavens" and the "light" we read about in Genesis represent the realm of pure spirits. (Physical light does not appear till several verses later, on the fourth day.) God created these angels of light, as he created everything, to be "good." Yet he also created them to be free, because only free creatures can experience love. Love cannot be coerced, or it ceases to be love. So God presented the angels with a decision, and some of them chose not to return his love. The book of Revelation seems to allude to this event, though in symbolic language, when it says that "a third of the stars of heaven" (12:4) were darkened (8:12) and cast down.

We do not know the nature of the angels' "test." Scripture doesn't say what it was, and the Church has made no definitive declaration on the matter. It's possible, too, that we could not even *begin* to understand the testing of pure spirits, whose knowledge is immediate and complete, and whose power far exceeds our own.

It is a subject that has fascinated many saints and theologians down the centuries. Many, in fact, have speculated that God infused all the angels with a foreknowledge of his incarnation. He revealed to them that he would create human beings—and that he would one day be united with humanity. God would become a man, and all the angels would have to adore the incarnate Word. The Letter to the Hebrews tells us: "When he brings the firstborn into the world, he says, 'Let all God's angels worship him'" (Hebrews 1:6, quoting Psalm 97:7).

Some of the angels, perhaps, judged God's commandment to be unreasonable and even insulting. In their pride and arrogance, they refused to worship a being that appeared to be so grossly inferior—even though God himself had commanded such worship!

It is interesting to note that in the book of Revelation the wicked angels fall from heaven immediately after God presents a vision of a mother with her child.

This is speculation, not dogma, but it is the speculation of some of God's closest friends among the saints. If their interpretation is correct, then we can understand why Christmas appears in the Gospels as an explosion of angelic activity. It would also explain why the devil was so enraged as to respond by bringing about the Slaughter of the Innocents and the flight of the Holy Family into Egypt (perhaps described symbolically in Revelation 12:4–6).

Christmas was the day of the good angels' vindication, and it marked the beginning of the devils' earthly comeuppance.

The firstborn had indeed come into the world, and all *God's* angels worshipped him.

Angels make their appearance at the very start of the Gospel story. The New Testament is dawning, yet we see it immediately as consonant and continuous with the Old Testament. The difference is in degree—we have moved from seed to flower, from foreshadowing to fulfillment. The same God presides over history, and he is moving his plan toward completion.

In the Old Testament, angels appear often, as do other pure spirits, such as watchers (Daniel 4:13), cherubim (Genesis 3:24), and seraphim (Isaiah 6:2). They serve as guardians and guides, messengers and catalysts. Angels rescue Hagar (Genesis 16) and visit judgment upon Sodom (Genesis 19). They "go before" Israel, leading the chosen people into the Holy Land (Exodus 32:34). They bring God's word to the prophets (1 Kings 13:18). Angels are mediators (Job 33:23), deliverers (Daniel 3:28), redeemers (Genesis 48:16), warriors (2 Chronicles 32:21), agents of creation (Psalm 104:4), and agents of destruction (2 Samuel 24:16).

No matter what the angels were doing, however, they were simultaneously *worshipping*. When Jesus spoke about guardian angels, he emphasized that even as they were guarding "little ones" they were also worshipping the Father in heaven (see Matthew 18:10). Worship is the primary activity of all pure spirits. Worship is what angels do.

For that reason, the Old Testament often associates the angels with the sacrificial cult. When Abraham goes to Mount Moriah to offer his son Isaac as a sacrifice, an angel is there to stay his hand. When the prophets Isaiah and Ezekiel are carrying out their priestly service in the Temple, they see visions of angels in the sanctuary (Isaiah 6:1–3; Ezekiel 9:3). Angels ascend to heaven with the flames and smoke of the sacrifices placed on Israel's altars (Judges 13:20). Images of the cherubim were, by divine command, placed in the holy of holies of Israel's tabernacle and Jerusalem's Temple.

So maybe we shouldn't be surprised, at the beginning of Saint Luke's Gospel, to find an angel appearing in the Temple to a priest named Zechariah, who is simply doing what priests do. He is offering incense at the appropriate altar when the angel appears. The angel brings him good news: Zechariah's wife, Elizabeth, who has been infertile all her life, will bring forth a child—and not just any child, but a prophet "great before the Lord" (Luke 1:11–17).

The angel even identifies himself by name—something only three angels do in all of the Bible. He is Gabriel, a figure Zechariah would have recognized from the book of Daniel (8:16; 9:21), where he was associated with the prophecies of the advent of the Messiah—specifically, the prophecies that calculated the years remaining till Christmas.

Zechariah, however, is not sufficiently impressed, and he dares to question the credibility of God's messenger (and, implicitly, God's message). For that he is struck mute and deaf.

The angel then goes to the home of Mary, a kinswoman of Zechariah, to tell her that she will conceive by the power of the Holy Spirit and bear the Messiah, the Christ, into the world. Mary believes the angel and accepts his word.

Thus the adventure of Christmas begins through the ministry of angels.

And thus it continues. This quality—the constancy of angelic presence—is evident in the accounts of both Matthew and Luke.

When Joseph was troubled by the knowledge of Mary's pregnancy, "an angel of the Lord appeared to him in a dream, saying, 'Joseph, son of David, do not fear to take Mary your wife, for that which is conceived in her is of the Holy Spirit'" (Matthew 1:20). The angel revealed to Joseph that the baby was the Savior of Israel. And Joseph did as the angel instructed (Matthew 1:24).

When the time arrived for the baby's birth, angels announced the occasion—not to the mighty, but to the humblest of people.

> And in that region there were shepherds out in the field, keeping watch over their flock by night. And an angel of the Lord appeared to them, and the glory of the Lord shone around them, and they were filled with fear. And the angel said to them, "Be not afraid; for behold, I bring you good news of a great joy which will come to all the people; for to you is born this day in the city of David a Savior, who is Christ the Lord. And this will be a sign for you: you will find a babe wrapped in swaddling cloths and lying in a manger." (Luke 2:8–12)

Yet, again, the angels didn't just carry out an earthly task. They worshipped, too. "And suddenly there was with the angel a multitude of the heavenly host praising God and saying, 'Glory to God in the highest, and on earth peace among men with whom he is pleased!'" (Luke 2:13–14). The angels gave glory and praise to God—in Bethlehem.

In Bethlehem! What the Old Testament prophets had seen happening in heaven was now taking place on earth. What the angels once did in the holy of holies in the Temple, they now were doing in a little town some distance from the holy city.

A gathering of angels is a clear and unmistakable sign of God's presence and his favor. For both Matthew and Luke, the angels of Christmas are a sign that God is present among his people in Jesus Christ. Jesus is Emmanuel, God with us (Matthew 1:23).

As the Christmas story played out, angels continued to play important roles. They were involved in the naming of the baby (Luke 2:21). They informed Joseph of Herod's plot to kill Jesus (Matthew 2:13). They instructed the Holy Family to flee to Egypt (Matthew 2:13–14). And they instructed them on when they could safely return from Egypt (Matthew 2:19–21).

The Gospels tell the Christmas story in historical terms. The book of Revelation tells it in symbols. But neither the Gospels nor the Apocalypse can tell the story truthfully without angels. It is angels who sing the Gloria. It is angels who announce the joy.

The angelic dimension of Christmas is not confined to the event or to the season. What happened in Bethlehem didn't stay in Bethlehem. It changed the world. It changed history. It changed the very structure of the cosmos.

It changed the way human beings relate to angels. Throughout the Old Testament, when angels appear to human beings, the typical response of the human is to fall to the ground. Lot did it (Genesis 19:1). Balaam did it (Numbers 22:31), as did Manoah and his wife (Judges 13:20). Even a prophet as good and virtuous as Daniel fell with his face to the ground when an angel appeared (Daniel 8:17; 10:9).

In the Old Testament, when a man fell down before an angel, the angel was likely to leave him there. In the New Testament, things changed a bit. When the angel appeared to Mary, she was clearly "troubled," yet the angel spoke to her deferentially, as a knight might speak to his queen. Nor do the angels seem to frighten Joseph or overwhelm him. Angels minister to Jesus (Matthew 4:11). By the time we get to the Acts of the Apostles, we see ordinary Christians living on intimate terms with the angels (Acts 12:15; 10:3–8, 22, 30–33). The leaders of the Church enjoyed the assistance of the angels (Acts 8:26; 27:23–24).

Something had changed between believers and angels. Though angels remained as terrifying as ever to sinners (Acts 12:23), they appear almost as brothers to the members of the Church.

Christ made the difference—all the difference in the world and all the difference in heaven. When God became man, he brought about a marvelous exchange of gifts. He shared his nature with lowly flesh (2 Peter 1:4), and he assumed the weakness of our flesh (Philippians 2:5–8). Saint Paul spoke repeatedly of this marvelous exchange, saying: "Our Lord Jesus Christ, . . . though he was rich, yet for your sake he became poor, so that by his poverty you might become rich" (2 Corinthians 8:9).

The angels saw this take place. The *holy* angels were those who were willing to worship God as a humble baby soiling his diaper, lying in the feeding trough of a stable at the outskirts of a backwater village. The holy angels were those who were willing to follow God in his descent to earth and worship him *there*—here!—as they did in heaven.

In coming to earth, Jesus united heaven and earth in the praise of God's glory. Shepherds and angels were, ever afterward, singing from the same hymnal. The song the angels taught the herdsmen, the Gloria, is still part of the Church's ritual at Sunday Mass.

When Saint Paul told the Christmas story, he couldn't help but use the occasion to explain the changed relationship between human beings and angelic beings. He says, in chapter four of his letter to the Galatians, that in the Old Testament the angels were like babysitters of the nation of Israel.

I mean that the heir, as long as he is a child, is no better than a slave, though he is the owner of all the estate; but he is under guardians and trustees until the date set by the father. So with us; when we were children, we were slaves to the elemental spirits of the universe. (Galatians 4:1–3)

But then, Paul goes on to say, Christmas came and changed everything.

But when the time had fully come, God sent forth his Son, born of woman, born under the law, to redeem those who were under the law, so that we might receive adoption as sons. (Galatians 4:4–5)

And that's *how* Christmas changed everything. By establishing the conditions for our adoption as children of God—by bringing about a certain *identification* between man and God in Jesus Christ.

The Church is the Body of Christ, and as such it is both heavenly and earthly. The Church is the communion of saints, and it includes as members both angels and shepherds—cherubim and seraphim, and you, and me.

Mary and Joseph, as we see them in the Gospels, live with the angels as we should learn to live with the angels. In our time on earth we are practicing for life in heaven, and when we live in heaven we will be living with the angels as our nearest neighbors.

They are close to us now, as the Christmas story makes clear and as we learn from the Holy Family.

The Reverend Billy Graham once said that "Christians should never fail to sense the operation of an angelic glory."[2] That's true enough, and it's clearly the lesson of Christmas, when the angels first sang "Glory!" on the earth. Mary and Joseph lived with a constant awareness of the angels' presence.

But theirs was not merely an awareness. It was not passive. It was active, receptive, engaged, devoted. Mary conversed with her angel and even asked him questions. Joseph acted on what the angel told him.

Throughout the Christmas story, angels supply the Holy Family with guidance, protection, prayer, wisdom, promptings. The Holy Family is actively responsive to all of it.

This is a hallmark of biblical religion. God's people interact with angels. And we have to ask ourselves: Why are these scenes in the Bible? Why did God inspire the sacred authors to include so many conversations between human beings and angels?

The Christian tradition is clear about the matter: the

biblical figures model what the Church calls *devotion* to the holy angels. We live with the angels as friends. Mary and Joseph model such devotion for us.

People sometimes roll their eyes when preachers propose the Holy Family as a model for domestic life today. How are ordinary folks supposed to imitate a household in which one member was God, another was conceived without Original Sin, and the third was indisputably "righteous" all his life? Well, devotion and attentiveness to the holy angels is a good place for us to begin. If even Jesus, Mary, and Joseph needed supernatural help, how much more do we who hobble under the effects of our personal history, our limitations, and our sins? The good news is: we have all the supernatural help we need.

The word *angel* comes from the Greek *angelos*, which means "messenger." The Hebrew equivalent, *malakh*, also bears that dual meaning of "heavenly spirit" and "earthly messenger." So angels are all about communication. They want to help us draw closer together as families, and they can help us—as they helped the Holy Family—get our message through to one another in a kind and gentle way.

Good children of Israel depended on the guidance and protection of the angels. "My angel goes before you," God told the generation of the exodus (Exodus 23:23)—and that, in so many words, is what he proved to the Holy Family. It's what he now says to every family that lives in Christ.

Where God abides, the angels worship. Where two or three are gathered in Christ's name, God abides, and the angels worship. Where there is a marriage bond, there is God—within that family sacramentally—and there the angels gather and worship.

In such a family, every day can be an occasion for experiencing the joy of Christmas.

⚜

O LITTLE TOWN OF
BETHLEHEM

*E*NGLISH SPEAKERS USE THE word *bedlam* to describe a scene of uproar and confusion—but the word originated as a mispronunciation of *Bethlehem*. The Hospital of Saint Mary of Bethlehem, founded in the thirteenth century in London, England, is still in operation today and is Europe's oldest psychiatric institution. In its early centuries, it housed so many suffering people that it was a constant scene of pandemonium. Its name became synonymous with madness and mania. It's one of the ironies of history that we apply the same name to chaos that we apply to that "little town" that lies "still" in its "deep and dreamless sleep."

Yet, as we've seen in our study of the historical sources—from Josephus and the Dead Sea Scrolls to the Gospels—there was indeed a riot of anxious expectations in first-century Palestine. The notion was widespread that the time of the

Messiah was imminent. And there was no shortage of people who wished to take advantage of the situation for their own military, political, or economic advantage. Between Herod the Great (in the first century BC) and Simon bar Kochba just a century after Christ, there arose many pretenders amid a confusing array of false prophecies.

The expectations and claims were wildly divergent in many ways. But most of them centered on a single idea: the restoration of a king like David—someone with the virtue and might of David, the priestly bearing of David, and the blessing of God that David enjoyed.

We find the common sentiment expressed in a poem written shortly before the time of Herod the Great.

> *Behold, O Lord, and raise up unto them their king, the son of*
> *David,*
> *At the time that you foresee, O God, may he reign over Israel*
> *your servant;*
> *And gird him with strength, that he may shatter unrighteous*
> *rulers. . . .*
> *Wisely, righteously he shall thrust out sinners from the*
> *inheritance,*
> *He shall destroy the pride of the sinner as a potter's vessel. . . .*
> *He shall destroy the godless nations with the word of his*
> *mouth. . . .*
> *And he shall reprove sinners for the thoughts of their heart.*

And he shall gather together a holy people, whom he shall lead in
   righteousness,
And he shall judge the tribes of the people that has been sanctified
   by the Lord his God.[1]

As the poem makes clear, the common belief was that the Messiah would arise from the family of David. He would be a "son of David." Remember: God had promised a descendant whose reign would be everlasting: "When your days are fulfilled and you lie down with your fathers, I will raise up your offspring after you, who shall come forth from your body, and I will establish his kingdom. He shall build a house for my name, and I will establish the throne of his kingdom for ever" (2 Samuel 7:12–13).

By the time of Christ, there was a strong consensus that not only would the Messiah come from David's bloodline, but he would also be born in David's birthplace, Bethlehem. In John's Gospel, the Jewish leaders who oppose Jesus asked: "Has not the scripture said that the Christ is descended from David, and comes from Bethlehem, the village where David was?" (John 7:42). They thought that this requirement would disqualify Jesus, because they knew he had grown up in Nazareth. Little did they know. . . .

In the thousand years from David's childhood to Jesus's birth, Bethlehem had declined rather drastically—from a prosperous walled city to a sleepy little town. Nonetheless, it remained a focus of speculation about the Messiah.

It's easy to see why. The town's association with David was clear from Scripture: "David was the son of an Ephrathite of Bethlehem in Judah" (1 Samuel 17:12); and as king, moreover, he always favored his hometown, even after he established Israel's capital in Jerusalem.

Centuries after David's death, God, through the prophet Micah, confirmed the promise—and *specified* that the anointed heir would arise from David's birthplace.

> *But you, O Bethlehem Ephrathah,*
> *who are little to be among the clans of Judah,*
> *from you shall come forth for me*
> *one who is to be ruler in Israel,*
> *whose origin is from of old,*
> *from ancient days. (Micah 5:2)*

From the New Testament we can see that these details were very important to the early Christians. The apostles and evangelists were faithful children of Israel, after all, and they had seen God's promises fulfilled. Saint Matthew cites Micah's prophecy and relates it to the birth of Jesus. Saint Luke also draws the connections between Jesus, King David, and Bethlehem. Joseph takes his pregnant wife to "the city of David, which is called Bethlehem, because he was of the house and lineage of David" (Luke 2:4).

To be born in Bethlehem was a mark of the Messiah. It was expected. And in Jesus the expectation was fulfilled.

❀

It is a census that draws Joseph to the town of his ancestors. But God orchestrates the event by means of decrees from far-off Rome and the bureaucratic machinery of provincial Syria. Saint Luke provides specific historical markers, noting that Quirinius was governor of Syria and Augustus was Caesar.

That exactitude has actually proven to be a stumbling block to some historians, who claim that the details don't jibe with the facts of Roman history as we know them from other sources. It's said that Augustus never ordered an empire-wide census, and that the census of the Roman governor of Syria, Quirinius, did not take place till AD 6. If Caesar's decree is historically suspect, they ask, and if Quirinius's census is chronologically too late to have brought Joseph and Mary to Bethlehem, can we even be sure that Jesus was born in David's hometown?

First things first. It's quite possible that Augustus ordered "enrollments" for which only minimal evidence has survived. We know that Augustus demanded registrations of different kinds at various points during his reign. The Jewish historian Josephus recounts that during the last years of Herod's rule, Judea was required to swear an oath of loyalty to Caesar. Archaeological evidence confirms that the same type of oath was sworn elsewhere in the empire around 3 BC. This might well mean that the registration described in Luke 2:1 involved an oath of allegiance sworn to the emperor—not a census taken for the purpose of taxation. A later Christian historian named Orosius (fifth century AD) says explicitly that Augustus required every person in every Roman province to be enrolled with a public oath. His description of the event strongly suggests that this oath was required in the years just before 2 BC, when the Roman people hailed Augustus as the first of all men. Caesar Augustus tells us in his personal writings that the whole Roman world had professed him to be the "Father" of the empire by the time this title was officially given to him in 2 BC. These converging lines of evidence make it possible that the census of Luke 2 was not a registration of residents to be taxed, but a public enrollment of subjects expressing their loyalty to the reigning emperor.

The role of Quirinius also presents a difficulty—though perhaps one that can be overcome. Quirinius is known from other historical sources. We know that he oversaw a taxation census soon after he was appointed as provincial legate of Syria in AD 6. Yet we do not know, given the current state of evidence, whether he held this office more than once or that he ever conducted more than one census.

How, then, can we square the career of Quirinius with a census that occurred many years earlier? This calls, I think, for a close reading of Luke's text.

The Greek expression he uses in Luke 2:2 for the governing role of Quirinius is the exact description he uses for Pontius Pilate's governing role in Luke 3:1. Since Pilate governed as a regional procurator and was not the legate of an entire Roman province (like Syria), it leaves open the possibility that Luke is referring to an administrative role assumed by Quirinius that had nothing to do with his later position as an imperial legate. One of the earliest Church Fathers, Justin Martyr, seems to provide support for this hypothesis. He tells us that Quirinius was a "procurator" in Judea (not Syria) at the time of Jesus's birth! Recall that Justin lived in Palestine less than a century after the events of Jesus's life. It would have been relatively easy for him to check facts; and, because he was an apologist, he usually addressed himself to opponents, who would have been eager to note his errors.

Justin's testimony, given in the second century, is at least as reliable a guide to events of the first century as the conjectures of historians in the twenty-first. He had access to monumental inscriptions and documentary records that have long since been reduced to rubble and dust.

Justin also enables us to make greater sense of the testimony of another early Christian writer, Tertullian of Carthage, who says that Saturninus (not Quirinius) was the official legate of Syria at the time of Jesus's birth. It may be that Quirinius was the administrator of a Judean census (such as the 3 BC oath registration) several years before he conducted another census for taxation in AD 6.

The early Christians were convinced that Jesus was the Son of David. All four Gospels attest to this, as do the letters of Saint Paul (see, for example, Romans 1:3 and 2 Timothy 2:8). They were convinced, furthermore, that he was born in Bethlehem. We have already noted that by the middle of the first century many Christians were making pilgrimages to the site of Jesus's birth.

Because of that devotion, and because of the prophecies, the little town of Bethlehem continued to exercise an outsized influence on the outside world. Around AD 135, the Romans built a shrine to one of their gods in the cave of the nativity. It is likely that this was done to stanch the flow of pilgrims to the site—since Christians had a horror of pagan idols. The Romans maintained the shrine there until the reign of Constantine in the fourth century.

The tradition of the Davidic Messiah was well known, even outside Israel. One ancient historian records that at the end of the first century AD, the Roman emperor Domitian still feared that a "Son of David" would arise as his rival. So he had the remnant of David's family rounded up and interrogated, but found them to be so impoverished as to be harmless.[2]

The Messiah born to Israel took everyone by surprise. The psalm of Solomon, quoted at the beginning of this chapter, foresaw that the Son of David would "thrust out sinners from the inheritance"—but who knew that he would accomplish this by forgiving sinners of their sins? The psalm foretold that the Son of David would "shatter unrighteous rulers"—but who knew that he would shatter their unrighteousness through a conversion of heart?

The emperor Domitian, in the end, was unimpressed. But millions of Romans believed in the event of Christmas, and it was not long before the Son of David ruled the hearts of a majority of the empire's subjects.

God's kingdom extended wherever the King, Jesus, was present in his Church. As King, Jesus reigns in the Eucharist. And the early Church Fathers delighted in pointing out that even this was foreshadowed by his birth in Bethlehem.

Beth Lechem in Hebrew means "house of bread." How fitting that in Bethlehem the "Bread of Life" should first be manifest to the world. Jesus said to them, "I am the bread of life. . . . I am the bread which came down from heaven" (John 6:35, 41).

The Dominican scholar Jerome Murphy-O'Connor, who dedicated his life to biblical archaeology, often said that Jesus's birth in Bethlehem was indisputable, and that its importance was hard to exaggerate: "If the early Church thought of Jesus in terms of Davidic messianism—and it certainly did—it was not because of anything he said or did but because of who he was and where he came from. And he came from Bethlehem."[3]

᠅

CHAPTER

9

DO YOU BELIEVE IN MAGI?

*I*F THERE WAS NO love lost between Israel and Persia
during the reign of King Herod, it's because there was so
little love to lose. Persia, a powerful empire, had been a peri-
odic oppressor of the Jews. In the first century BC, moreover,
Persia was experiencing the first blush of what would prove
to be a centuries-long power struggle with that upstart on the
geopolitical scene: Rome.

If the Jews and Romans agreed on anything, it was on their
contempt for Persia, the empire to the east. And for both Jews
and Romans, Persia's loathsomeness was best symbolized by
its "wise men," or Magi. For the Roman naturalist Pliny the
Elder (a contemporary of Jesus), the doctrine of the Magi was
"so utterly incredible, so utterly revolting," yet so full of "attractive chimeras," that it was capable of "fascinating men's

minds."[1] Centuries later, the Talmud acknowledged the same attractive power and forbade Jews to seek knowledge from a Magus (the singular of *Magi*).

The Magi were astronomers who closely tracked the movements of heavenly bodies—the relative position of the stars, the phases of the moon—and claimed to read them as omens of earthly events. Their doctrine "attained an influence so mighty," said Pliny, that it "held sway throughout a great part of the world, and ruled the kings of kings in the East."[2] The Magi were so revered in Persia that they were considered the true "power behind the throne" and were sometimes made vassal kings of provincial lands.

In the Old Testament, we find Magi—the word is usually translated as "wise men"—serving as advisors to the king in Babylon as well (see Daniel 2:48). One is listed among the eyewitnesses when King Nebuchadnezzar slaughtered the heirs of Israel's king David and then blinded their father, Zedekiah. Prominent among the names of Babylon's "officers" is Nergal-sharezer the Rabmag, or chief of the Magi (see Jeremiah 39:1–7).

Though the Magi were near neighbors to the Jews in geographic terms, religiously they were light-years away. In many ways they personified the world of the Gentiles—they were foreigners and idolaters who were ignorant and contemptuous of Israel's ways and Israel's God. They represented the kind of contamination the law was designed to keep out. God gave the law in order to quarantine the Israelites from the influence of idolatrous people.

So there was a mutual repulsion between the Magi and the Jews—yet there was also a mutual attraction. If Jews had never felt drawn to the wisdom of the Persians, there would have been no need for warnings in the Bible and the Talmud.

As for the Magi themselves: if they had never been tempted to know the God of Israel, why were they watching the sky for signs of a divine "King of the Jews"?

❧

Now when Jesus was born in Bethlehem of Judea in the days of Herod the king, behold, wise men from the East came to Jerusalem, saying, "Where is he who has been born king of the Jews? For we have seen his star in the East, and have come to worship him." (Matthew 2:1–2)

Now, we've already established that Herod was haunted by extreme paranoia. We know, too, that he was an insecure Edomite, reviled by Jews of purer lineage. Furthermore, we've seen that his paranoia and insecurity drove him to search the Scriptures for any hint of a threat to his power. Surely his researches had at some point brought him to one of the earliest prophecies of the Messiah, an oracle of Balaam, preserved in the Torah:

I see him, but not now;
I behold him, but not nigh:
a star shall come forth out of Jacob,
and a scepter shall rise out of Israel;
it shall crush the forehead of Moab,
and break down all the sons of Sheth.
Edom shall be dispossessed,
Se'ir also, his enemies, shall be dispossessed,
while Israel does valiantly.
By Jacob shall dominion be exercised,
and the survivors of cities be destroyed! (Numbers 24:17–19)

To a paranoid Edomite pretender, three lines would have stood out:

a star shall come forth out of Jacob,
and a scepter shall rise out of Israel;
. . . .
[and] Edom shall be dispossessed. (Numbers 24:17–18)

Could these Magi have seen the star foretold by Balaam? Could they have descried the omen of Herod's undoing?

It's possible, too, that the Magi knew the prophecy of Balaam from their interaction with Jews in Persia—and that they had seen its meaning far more clearly than the religious leaders of the Jews. Maybe that's the reason *why* they were on the lookout for such a star.

Herod pressed the Magi for details, and he called up the members of his own religious think tank. From these two sources he wanted to pinpoint the place and time of the Messiah's birth.

The Magi must have impressed Herod as humble seekers and virtuous men. So he tried his best to play-act humility. He told them: "Go and search diligently for the child, and when you have found him bring me word, that I too may come and worship him" (Matthew 2:8).

They went their way. "When they saw the star, they rejoiced exceedingly with great joy" (Matthew 2:10).

We should linger on that single line. For it captures the very moment when God gave "Joy to the World"—not merely to Israel, but to the whole world: the nations, the foreigners, the Gentiles.

All through the Old Testament there had been hints that such a day would come. The psalmist sang: "All the kings of the earth shall praise thee, O LORD, / for they have heard the words of thy mouth" (Psalm 138:4). And:

> *May the kings of Tarshish and of the isles*
> *render him tribute,*
> *may the kings of Sheba and Seba bring gifts! (Psalm 72:10)*

And the prophet Isaiah foretold a time when Israel would prosper, unafraid of the world and open to the gifts of the nations:

> *Then you shall see and be radiant,*
> *your heart shall thrill and rejoice;*
> *because the abundance of the sea shall be turned to you,*
> *the wealth of the nations shall come to you.*
>
> . . . .
>
> *Your gates shall be open continually;*
> *day and night they shall not be shut;*
> *that men may bring to you the wealth of the nations,*
> *with their kings led in procession. (Isaiah 60:5, 11)*

The Magi went to Jerusalem, and then to Bethlehem, and they were bearing tribute with them. Saint Matthew tells us: "Then, opening their treasures, they offered [Jesus] gifts, gold and frankincense and myrrh" (Matthew 2:11).

Christians have long pondered the meaning of the Magi's gifts. The great Scripture scholar of the third century Origen of Alexandria said succinctly: "Gold, as to a king; myrrh, as to one who was mortal; and incense, as to a God."[3] The symbolism makes the gifts particularly suitable to the baby who was at once king, man, and God.

Gold and incense are familiar to everyone, and their associations with kings and temples are well known; only myrrh requires an explanation for some modern readers. Myrrh is made from the fragrant resin of trees native to many lands in the Middle East. In ancient times, myrrh was used for medicines, perfumes, and—most significantly in this case—embalming fluid. The bodies of the dead were anointed with myrrh to slow decomposition and mask the odor of death (see John 19:39).

Origen's analysis serves as a good summary, but it's hardly the last word. Indeed, it's a necessary and good beginning for our contemplation, but it's only a beginning.

It is worth noting, for example, that all three gifts were customary elements of worship in Israel's holy place. In the Temple the vessels were crafted from purest gold (see Leviticus 24:4-6); the smoke of incense rose with the prayers of the priests (Leviticus 16:12-13); and myrrh was used in the oils for anointing (Exodus 30:23). Thus, we can see in this moment a transfer of high-priestly authority to its rightful place, with Israel's King Messiah, the Son of David.

Saint Ephrem the Syrian (fourth century) was delighted to note that all the gifts brought by the Magi had first been created by God. So the Magi were simply returning to God what he had first given to the world. The gifts, however, had been profaned by their service to idols in the lands of the Magi; so, said Saint Ephrem, they needed to be purified by contact with the Holy One of Israel.

The gold that had been worshipped
now worshipped you, when the magi offered it.
What had been worshipped in molten images,
now gave worship to you.
With its worshippers it worshipped you.[4]

And again, according to Saint Ephrem, the Magi brought more to Bethlehem than the gifts in their coffers. The Magi brought themselves, as representatives of all the Gentiles; and the Magi brought the whole cosmos, which they had striven to understand and had mistakenly worshipped. Ephrem was their countryman and was familiar with the fire worship of the Persians. But in Bethlehem, he said, "The Sun rendered worship" to the true God, as the Sun's "worshippers . . . worshipped" Christ instead.[5] When the Magi worshipped the Christ Child, the Sun was worshipping Jesus through the Magi.

The visit of the Magi is a brief episode in the Christmas story, but we cannot exaggerate its importance. It signals the salvation of the whole world and the restoration of the cosmic order, which had been disturbed with the fall of humanity and the angels.

The early Christians who had converted from idolatry, from "paganism," had a profound appreciation for the story of the Magi. It is cited repeatedly in the second century by authors as diverse and geographically dispersed as Saint Justin Martyr, Tatian, Julius Africanus, Saint Irenaeus of Lyons, and Tertullian of Carthage. It is found as well in the apocryphal Christian literature of the period.

God had extended joy to the world, and the world responded with worship and celebration.

And what of the star?

As far back as the fourth century, Saint John Chrysostom pointed out that it didn't behave like any other star anyone had ever seen. Most stars, he said, appear to move from east to west, like the sun; but this star "wafted from north to south; for so is Palestine situated with respect to Persia."

It appeared, moreover, burning bright at midday, Chrysostom added, "and this is not within the power of a star, nor even of the moon."

And he went on to give more reasons. The star played hide-and-seek with the Magi, Chrysostom said, guiding them to Jerusalem, and then disappearing for a time, and then reappearing. Again, it's clear that this was no ordinary star.

Finally, as the Magi approached their goal, the star descended from heaven and hovered above the Holy Family's house.

"This star," said Saint John Chrysostom, "was not of the common sort, or rather not a star at all, it seems to me, but some invisible power transformed into this appearance."[6]

In chapter 7 we saw that the stars in the sky were often identified with angels in heaven. The motif appears in the Bible, and in other Jewish sources from the time of Jesus. The philosopher Philo of Alexandria speculated that the stars "are living creatures, but of a kind composed entirely of mind."[7]

Brilliant scientists have spent years combing through ancient chronicles, reconciling calendars, and working out the equations—all so that they could identify the star of Bethlehem with a known astronomical phenomenon: Halley's Comet, for example, or some once-in-centuries conjunction of planets. Their arguments are ingenious, but I'm not persuaded.

John Chrysostom may have been pre-scientific and pre-critical in his thinking, but he wasn't stupid. He knew that stars *don't* do what the star of Bethlehem was said to do. I'm inclined to agree with him that this was yet another appearance of a Christmas angel. In the beginning, God had created the heavens and the earth, and all the angels were caught up in the cosmic drama. Now all find themselves, once again, caught up in its climax.

With John Chrysostom I have to conclude that an angel appeared to the Magi as light and led them to true worship—which, as I've said before, is what angels were created to do.

Pope Saint Gregory the Great accepted the angelic interpretation. He observed, too, the great difference between the way God dealt with the shepherds and the way he dealt with the Magi. The shepherds, even though they were uneducated Jews of the lowest rank, were still members of the chosen people, who had heard the proclamation of the truth all their lives. To them God sent angels undisguised, as it were, and the angels spoke to them in plain language. "But a sign and not a voice guided the gentiles," Gregory explained. "For they were not prepared to make full use of reason to know the Lord."[8]

To understand the meaning of Christmas, the simplest of pious field hands were better equipped than the most erudite scholars.

What brought the Magi to the crib in Bethlehem, however, was their ardent disposition to know the truth. That's something the angels could see—and work with.

Saint Matthew is maddeningly sketchy on details. If Luke had given us the story of the Magi, we would probably know their postal addresses in Persia. But all Matthew tells us is that they came from "the east."

Scripture doesn't tell us how many Magi there were. An ancient tradition tells us there were three, but that may have been inferred from the number of gifts. Other ancient traditions even give us names: Caspar (or Gaspar), Balthasar, and Melchior. But Scripture, again, is silent on these details. The

Gospel doesn't even disclose that they were Persian, though we assume that by the simple fact that they were Magi.

The culture's "insiders" didn't receive the message of the herald angels. The chief priests were busy with earthly matters in places far from Bethlehem. King Herod and his court were otherwise occupied with their intrigues and indulgence.

What we know about the Magi is mysterious but thrilling. The religious insiders of Herod's kingdom missed out on Christmas. But outsiders came from afar to pay homage.

Magi—Gentiles, foreigners, who were considered unclean by the Jews—arrived from distant lands, and they joined the worship of humble shepherds.

"And the master said . . . , 'Go out to the highways and hedges, and compel people to come in, that my house may be filled'" (Luke 14:23).

The Magi "rejoiced exceedingly with great joy" (Matthew 2:10).

CHAPTER

10

SHEPHERDS, WHY
THIS JUBILEE?

*I*T'S UNLIKELY THAT KING Herod would have been as
impressed with the testimony of shepherds as he was with
the opinions of the Magi. Shepherds had little wealth, power,
or even land that they could call their own. They dressed for
the elements, not for the banquet hall. And they smelled like
their sheep, as a shepherd should. Magi could gain an audience with King Herod. But shepherds? Probably not.

Maybe it would have been different in the courts of King
David. After all, he was a shepherd himself. He continued to
tend his father Jesse's flocks even as he rose in the ranks of the
military under King Saul (1 Samuel 17:15). When the time
came for David to be made king, the Lord says through his
prophet: "You shall be shepherd of my people Israel, and you
shall be prince over Israel" (2 Samuel 5:2; see also 1 Chronicles 11:2).

David never forgot his origins; and, in the most famous song he wrote, he praised God not as a mighty king, but as a shepherd!

> *The LORD is my shepherd, I shall not want;*
> *he makes me lie down in green pastures.*
> *He leads me beside still waters;*
> *he restores my soul.*
> *He leads me in paths of righteousness*
> *for his name's sake. (Psalm 23:1–3)*

David dares to pray to God as the Divine Shepherd—a God who leads, feeds, tends, restores, protects, refreshes, and provides for the people he has chosen as his "sheep."

Salvation, for David, was wrapped up in God's good shepherding:

> *O save your people, and bless your heritage;*
> *be their shepherd, and carry them for ever. (Psalm 28:9)*

Nor were these terms new with David. The Hebrews were herdsmen from their origin. Abraham lived a nomadic life, wandering with his flocks from Ur of the Chaldeans to the lands God had promised him. In fact, even before Abraham, at the dawn of humanity, the Torah identified Abel the herdsman as the righteous man of his generation.

In time, Jacob was mingling with shepherds when he spied Rachel, his beloved (Genesis 29:1). Noble Joseph, the patriarch and dreamer, was named as a shepherd (Genesis 37:2). The Hebrews' identity as shepherds even protected them, for a while, from the Egyptians, who had a horror of the trade (see Genesis 46:34). The book of Genesis ends with the patriarch Jacob's blessing upon his sons, in which he refers to God as "the Shepherd" (Genesis 49:24).

Israel's vocation to herding resumes immediately after their years of enslavement in Egypt. Moses is tending flocks when he's called to be his people's deliverer (Exodus 3:1). The journey described in the book of Exodus is defined by shepherding, as God tells Israel: "Your children shall be shepherds in the wilderness forty years" (Numbers 14:33).

The identity would be enduring, and flocks of sheep provide the dominant metaphors for Israel's self-understanding. When the people sin, they go "astray" (Psalm 119:67), as sheep do, and are "scattered upon the mountains, as sheep that have no shepherd" (1 Kings 22:17). Leaders are discussed as good or bad "shepherds." David appears, then, as the archetype of the "good shepherd" of his people.

Israel waited long centuries for another shepherd like David to arise. Through the prophets God promised: "I will give you shepherds after my own heart, who will feed you with knowledge and understanding" (Jeremiah 3:15). And the prophet Ezekiel foretold that the Good Shepherd would be born from the House of David: "My servant David shall be king over them; and they shall all have one shepherd. They shall follow my ordinances and be careful to observe my statutes" (Ezekiel 37:24, written long after David's death).

Thus the study of Israel's shepherds is a genealogy of its redeemers: Abraham, Jacob, Joseph, Moses, and David. All had their flaws and foreshadowed the Messiah still to come.

It should come as no surprise, then, for us to find shepherds at the birth of Jesus. All through history God had shown them favor.

Yet the religious and political leaders of Jesus's time had little use for them. A shepherd's work required constancy, and his time in the field often kept him from observing the hundreds of laws for ritual purity imposed by the Pharisees. It was a commonplace notion in Jesus's day that only the rich could afford the leisure to keep the law—and therefore be saved. Jesus shocks his hearers when he says: "It is easier for a camel to go through the eye of a needle than for a rich man to enter the kingdom of God" (Luke 18:25). The bystanders respond by crying out: "Then who can be saved?"

You can be fairly certain that the shepherds in pastures outside Bethlehem were not on anyone's short list of "the saved."

Shepherds lived their lives outdoors, often in contact with

the blood and droppings of the animals they tended. Shepherds were filthy, unlike the elite members of the Pharisee party or the effete members of Herod's court.

Yet it was to shepherds—and not to the king or the priests—that God sent the birth announcement for his only Son.

And in that region there were shepherds out in the field, keeping watch over their flock by night. And an angel of the Lord appeared to them, and the glory of the Lord shone around them, and they were filled with fear. And the angel said to them, "Be not afraid; for behold, I bring you good news of a great joy which will come to all the people; for to you is born this day in the city of David a Savior, who is Christ the Lord. And this will be a sign for you: you will find a babe wrapped in swaddling cloths and lying in a manger."

And suddenly there was with the angel a multitude of the heavenly host praising God and saying, "Glory to God in the highest, and on earth peace among men with whom he is pleased!"

When the angels went away from them into heaven, the shepherds said to one another, "Let us go over to Bethlehem and see this thing that has happened, which the Lord has made known to us." And they went with haste, and found Mary and Joseph, and the babe lying in a manger. And when they saw it they made known the saying which had been told them concerning this child; and all who heard it wondered at what the shepherds told them. But Mary kept all these things, pondering them in her heart. And the shepherds returned, glorifying and praising God for all they had heard and seen, as it had been told them. (Luke 2:8–20)

God sent not just one angel to the shepherds, but an army, a heavenly host, as he had sent to Jacob and Joshua in their times of need (see Genesis 28:12; 32:1–2; Joshua 5:13–15). As in the times of Jacob and Joshua, the nativity was a time of conquest—and the righteous on earth required the help of the angels of heaven.

The humble shepherds surely were awestruck by the sight. Perhaps they had heard of such visions taking place in the sanctuary of the Temple, where only the priests could serve—but not in a pungent pasture outside Bethlehem—and certainly not to shepherds!

The angels taught the shepherds a song that the Church has never forgotten: "Glory to God in the highest, and on earth peace among men with whom he is pleased." The ancient *Liber Pontificalis* (Book of the Popes) tells us that the song has been part of the Church's liturgy since the earliest times and was mandated for Christmas Mass by Pope Saint Telesphorus (circa AD 126).[1]

And the song is appropriate because, we are told, "the

glory of the Lord shone around" the angelic presence. This "glory" was not a simple radiance. It had a precise meaning for pious Jews. It represented the Shekinah, the bright and fiery "glory cloud," that filled the holy of holies in the tabernacle and the Temple (see Exodus 40:35; 2 Chronicles 7:2), but that had been absent since the time of the first Temple's destruction. The Shekinah was the visible sign of God's invisible presence.

Again, the shepherds had surely heard of such things happening to the priests in the Jerusalem Temple—but not to shepherds in Bethlehem.

To the poor comes the "good news" of salvation: "a Savior, who is the Lord Messiah." Thus the outcasts are the first to receive the Gospel, and they are the first, in turn, to evangelize the world: "The shepherds returned, glorifying and praising God for all they had heard and seen, as it had been told them."

The account of the shepherds ends on a note of wonder, glory, and praise. This is a reader's first glimpse of the *joy* that's a hallmark of Saint Luke's Gospel (see Luke 2:20; 5:26; 7:16; 13:13; 17:15; 18:43; 24:53). The joy given to a few must be brought to the world, beginning with those closest to home. The shepherds, then, appear as models of joyful evangelizing.

Jesus is a king far greater than Herod or Augustus. Yet he did not build a palace in Jerusalem; instead he made his dwelling in a humble cave in Bethlehem. He chose humble shepherds as his first courtiers.

He would identify himself with shepherds all his life, calling himself the Good Shepherd (John 10:11–14) and looking at the mass of humanity as his flock. "When he saw the crowds, he had compassion for them, because they were harassed and helpless, like sheep without a shepherd" (Matthew 9:36).

As we learned from the genealogies, the nativity is a recapitulation of so much that has gone before. The figure of the shepherd reprises many great events from Israel's history: the creation, the call of Abraham, the exodus, the kingdom, and the exile. Most poignantly the nativity of Jesus harks back to the reign of King David. David was a true shepherd and a skilled one—in both the literal and figurative senses—but he was still flawed and he failed his flock. When he failed, God chastised him in terms a shepherd would understand, referring to David's victim, Uriah the Hittite, as a "ewe lamb" (2 Samuel 12:3).

Yet to David, God promised a son who would be God's Son, too. He would be a good shepherd to his people. And the news would go first to David's colleagues in the pastures— and then outward, as joy, to the world.

THE GLORY OF YOUR PEOPLE: THE PRESENTATION

O UTSIDE THE GOSPELS OF Matthew and Luke, the New Testament alludes only briefly—in a glancing way—to Jesus's birth. We've already seen the dramatic, cosmic, symbolic rendering found in the book of Revelation. Saint Paul's version is far more understated, but just as theologically rich.

> But when the time had fully come, God sent forth his Son, born of woman, born under the law, to redeem those who were under the law, so that we might receive adoption as sons. (Galatians 4:4–5)

The God who had given the law—through angels, to Moses, for Israel—was now submissive to the law. By taking flesh as a Jew, he bound himself to a particular people, and he underwent the initiation required of them since the time of Abraham. Luke tells us: "And at the end of eight days, when he was circumcised, he was called Jesus, the name given by the angel before he was conceived in the womb" (Luke 2:21). Israel's covenant with God was "the covenant of circumcision" (Acts 7:8); and, though Jesus, as God, was not bound by the law, only he could fulfill the law perfectly, precisely because he was God and therefore sinless. And so he did, as his parents took him to be circumcised, perhaps at the synagogue in Bethlehem.

Christians have always seen this moment as an anticipation of Jesus's crucifixion. It was the first shedding of his blood, whose value was infinite. Because of Jesus's perfection, this rite by itself possessed power enough to redeem the world; yet he pressed on to a more perfect fulfillment and more complete self-giving. To his own law he would be obedient—"obedient unto death" (Philippians 2:8).

Circumcision customarily took place on the eighth day, and it was certainly demanding of the child. The law's next ritual took place on the fortieth day, and was demanding on the parents. After Mary's ordeal of giving birth in a distant place—and in a stable, no less!—the Holy Family took up another journey, to Jerusalem.

The son of Mary and Joseph was the Son of David, the great priest-king, so Jerusalem was his birthright. At David's capital, the walls of Jerusalem enclosed the "City of the Great King" (Mount Zion, see Matthew 5:35) as well as the Temple Mount. Jerusalem was the place of David's rule and the place of his rites—the privileged home of the monarch but, more important, the sanctuary of God's presence on earth.

For these reasons, Jerusalem is important in all the Gospel narratives, but in none does the sacrificial cult hold such prominence as it does in the Gospel according to Saint Luke. Remember, Luke is depicted symbolically as an ox for this reason: the ox was commonly offered as sacrifice. Luke begins his Gospel narrative in the Temple's holy place, when the archangel Gabriel appeared to Zechariah the priest. For Luke, the story line always finds its way back to Jerusalem and the Temple.

The ancient law accommodated his purpose. The Torah prescribed that every woman who gave birth should, forty days afterward, make a pilgrimage to the Temple for "purification." Every firstborn, moreover, must accompany her and be "redeemed"—bought back—like an unclean donkey. The comparison may seem offensive, but it is in the biblical text itself: "Every firstling of an ass you shall redeem with a lamb, or if you will not redeem it you shall break its neck. Every first-born of man among your sons you shall redeem" (Exodus 13:13).

Luke's narrative is quite odd. He describes Jesus not as being "redeemed," but rather as being "dedicated" or "presented" in the Temple. It's an important difference.[1] The law did not require the *presentation* of each firstborn. The book of Exodus required that all firstborn males be *redeemed*.

What's going on here? Luke seems to be portraying Jesus as a holy firstborn Israelite with a natural priestly status.[2] Luke's quotation concerning the firstborn (Luke 2:23) is based not on the law concerning redemption (Exodus 13:13), but rather on Exodus 13:1–2, which deals with the *consecration of the firstborn to the Lord*.

> The LORD said to Moses, "Consecrate to me all the firstborn; whatever is the first to open the womb among the people of Israel, both of man and of beast, is mine."

Luke, in fact, records no redemption ritual being performed for Jesus.[3] Jesus was not ransomed, and this was not at all normal. The New Testament scholar Charles Talbert is one of many who have made note of this anomaly.

> The prescription of Exodus 13:2 concerning the first-born son was literally fulfilled in the case of Jesus, the first-born (Luke 2:7), who was not ransomed (Exodus 13:13; Numbers 3:47; 18:16). Contrary to normal custom, Jesus was dedicated to God and remained his property. . . . *The*

closest parallel to this emphasis is found in 1 Samuel 1–2,
where Hannah gives Samuel, at his birth, to the Lord for
as long as the child lives. . . . If Jesus, in a similar manner,
was dedicated to God and not redeemed, he belonged to
God permanently. This would explain the reason Jesus
would not understand why his parents did not know where
to find him in Jerusalem (2:48–49): since he was God's he
could be expected to be in his Father's house, as in the
case of Samuel. At the plot level of the narrative, Jesus
had made a personal identification with the decisions his
parents had made about him at his birth.[4]

Thus, Luke presents Jesus as a uniquely righteous firstborn, who—unlike other Israelite males—did not need to be
redeemed from service to the Lord, since he was not unclean.
Instead, he was *consecrated as a firstborn* (Exodus 13:1–2).[5]

According to the Epistle to the Hebrews, this is why God
exalts Christ as his firstborn Son (1:6) and as a High Priest
and King (5:6; 6:20; 7:11, 17). Jesus goes up to Jerusalem to
fulfill the priestly covenant in such a way as to conclude it, yet
also to *in*clude it in God's covenant with the House of David.[6]
Jesus, the Anointed One, is the sole heir to the priesthood as
well as the monarchy. He recovers for mankind the dominion
and priesthood that Adam received from God, but then for-
feited by committing the original sin.

Yet it's not a simple restoration. God goes one better than

that. In Christ, humanity doesn't simply *revert* to an earthly paradise like Eden; rather it is *converted* upward—"to the assembly [church] of the first-born who are enrolled in heaven" (Hebrews 12:23).

Our friend Saint Luke is one of the authors often associated with the composition of the Epistle to the Hebrews, and it's easy to see why. The themes introduced in the third Gospel—of sacrifice, sanctuary, and priesthood—are developed profoundly in that letter. What begins in the earthly Temple finds its conclusion in Hebrews in the heavenly Church.

When Christ enters the Temple for his presentation, he enters as the rightful High Priest, and with the presentation he is consecrated for that role. He arrives as the long-awaited priest. He is also the sacrifice. He, indeed, as his life will show, is the true Temple (see John 2:19–21).

There was a second rite required forty days after a child was born, and that one was prescribed for the mother. The law required the child's mother to offer sacrifice for the sake of purification after childbirth.

This does not mean (as modern readers sometimes misread this passage) that the law considered sex or womanhood or childbirth to be "dirty" or sinful. No, just as the priest had to purify the holy vessels every time they were used in the

Temple liturgy (after pouring wine libations, for example, or splashing sacrificial blood upon the altar), so a woman who gave birth also had to be purified following the holy use of her sacred body (in giving birth to a new child).

Purification at once acknowledges the holiness of the vessel and renews that holiness so that it can once again carry out God's sacred purposes. After the vessels are purified, they may be used again by the priests in the sacred liturgy of the Temple; after forty days, the woman's body is purified so that she can be united with her husband in marital communion. The profound analogy between the Temple and the body is very important to understand, here and elsewhere in Scripture (see John 2:19–21; 1 Corinthians 3:16; 6:19; 7:14–15; 2 Corinthians 4:7; 5:1–10; 6:14–7:1).

Blood, moreover, was rightly considered a life force (see Leviticus 17:11). As such it was—like life itself—a gift from God. It was said to "defile" a body the way the scrolls of Scripture (according to the ancient rabbis) "defiled" the hands that touched them.[7] Human beings who have contact with the holy are made profoundly aware of their unworthiness, as we see many times in the Scriptures (see, for example, Daniel 8:17–18; Luke 5:8).

Mary was sinless. She was "full of grace." In no way did she need to be cleansed of sin. Yet she knew that grace was a divine gift she could never merit on her own. In her humility, she submitted to the law requiring purification.

While the Holy Family was at the Temple for the rites, they encountered an old man and an old woman, Simeon and Anna. The appearance of each was brief, but significant.

Anna, Saint Luke tells us, was from the tribe of Asher, one of the northern tribes that had for centuries been lost in dispersion. Her presence in the Temple, welcoming the Messiah, signaled the restoration of all of Israel as it had been constituted under King David. She is identified as a prophetess—and indeed she saw things as they really were, not merely as they appeared. She proclaimed Jesus as the redeemer (Luke 2:36, 38).

Simeon, too, heralded Jesus as Savior—and not only to Israel, but to "all peoples, a light for revelation to the Gentiles" (Luke 2:31–32).

Yet not all was sweetness and light. Simeon also turned to Mary and told her: "Behold, this child is set for the fall and rising of many in Israel, and for a sign that is spoken against (and a sword will pierce through your own soul also), that thoughts out of many hearts may be revealed" (Luke 2:35).

Salvation had come; but the work of salvation would be an ordeal for both mother and child.

FLIGHT INTO JOY

*M*Y WIFE, *KIMBERLY, AND* I have family far flung in the United States. My mother lives in the next state over from us. Kimberly's parents have made a home out west, as has our second son with his growing family. Our eldest son and his brood live in the Midwest; and our only daughter lives with her husband and son in a state along the East Coast.

So, for the Hahns, Christmas means travel, with all of its attendant busyness and bother. In our highly mobile society, that's what Christmas means to more and more people every year.

That is just as it should be. Families *should* make an effort to get together for holy days. And Christmas, after all, would be the appropriate time. It's the feast whose biblical backstory involves the most mileage.

Think about it.

- The story had hardly begun when Mary, pregnant with Jesus, went from Nazareth to the Judean hill country to serve her kinfolk, Zechariah and Elizabeth, in their need.
- At some point she must have made a return trip to Nazareth.
- When she was almost at her due date, Mary and Joseph traveled from Nazareth to Bethlehem to enroll for the census.
- Forty days after the baby's birth, the family went from Bethlehem to Jerusalem for the sacred rites of purification and consecration.

The Holy Family didn't move as many *miles* as the Hahns usually do, but they certainly knew more hardship. Planes, trains, and automobiles all provide irritating moments when we're in transit, but they're much more comfortable than a donkey trying to make its way over rough dirt roads.

And those four journeys were only the beginning for Jesus, Mary, and Joseph. When the Holy Family had finished up their sacred obligations in Jerusalem, they faced their most daunting itinerary of all—a trip that must have taken them completely by surprise.

❧

When the Magi failed to return to Herod, the king grew mad with rage. Assuming that they had found the newborn contender for his throne—and knowing that the Messiah was to be born in Bethlehem—"he sent and killed all the male children in Bethlehem and in all that region who were two years old or under" (Matthew 2:16).

Christian tradition refers to this as the Massacre of the Innocents. Skeptics note that the event appears in none of the other chronicles of Herod's reign. But that should not surprise us, really. His horrific acts were many, and most are recorded in only one source (usually Josephus). Even in Josephus, the catalog is representative rather than exhaustive. The Jewish historian chose the events that, for him, were most characteristic of the despot. But the victims of the Bethlehem massacre were relatively few in number. Bethlehem was a small town, and it's possible that the massacre involved no more than six victims, all from families of little social standing. In a reign like Herod's, it would have been one of the lesser massacres and unlikely to attract the attention of historians.

Yet it fits with what we know about Herod. He was

homicidal, insecure to the point of paranoia, and he had no compunction about killing people. You've already gotten a sense of the body count. He murdered one of his wives and three of his sons. He slaughtered the Jerusalem priests whose scriptural interpretations made him anxious, and his other sporadic purges claimed victims by the hundreds.

What are a few dead infants and toddlers to such a man?

Historians perhaps could ignore the purge, but it left an impression on the local populace. Saint Matthew conveys the extreme sorrow with a lament from the Old Testament:

Then was fulfilled what was spoken by the prophet Jeremiah:

> *"A voice was heard in Ramah,*
> *wailing and loud lamentation,*
> *Rachel weeping for her children;*
> *she refused to be consoled,*
> *because they were no more." (Matthew 2:17–18)*

The Church has always remembered these youngest victims of Herod as martyrs, from the Greek word *martus,* meaning "witness in a court of law." Like all such witnesses, the Holy Innocents died *in odium fidei,* because of the hatred of the faith. By their death they bore testimony to Jesus as the

Messiah. The feast memorializing them has been on Christian calendars since the time of the early Church, always celebrated in the week after Christmas (currently on December 28, unless the date falls on a Sunday). At Masses on that day our priests wear red vestments to commemorate the blood that was shed for Christ.

It is a miracle that Christ's blood was not mingled with that of his infant contemporaries. Saint Matthew (our only source for the story) presents Jesus's rescue in dramatic terms, as an angelic intervention requiring immediate action.

> Now when they had departed, behold, an angel of the Lord appeared to Joseph in a dream and said, "Rise, take the child and his mother, and flee to Egypt, and remain there till I tell you; for Herod is about to search for the child, to destroy him." And he rose and took the child and his mother by night, and departed to Egypt, and remained there until the death of Herod. This was to fulfill what the Lord had spoken by the prophet, "Out of Egypt have I called my son." . . .
>
> But when Herod died, behold, an angel of the Lord appeared in a dream to Joseph in Egypt, saying, "Rise,

take the child and his mother, and go to the land of
Israel, for those who sought the child's life are dead."
(Matthew 2:13–15, 19–20)

The event is rich in resonance. The Old Testament echoes
often in these first chapters of the New Testament. In this
story we find Jesus retracing the steps of Israel as they entered the dark period of their slavery under the Egyptian pharaoh. Saint Matthew quotes the prophet Hosea (11:1): "Out of
Egypt have I called my son." Thus we see that Hosea points
back to Israel's exodus, but also forward to Jesus's exile. Jesus
is, moreover, identified as God's "son"—prefigured by the
nation of Israel, but now fulfilled in the Christ.

Egypt holds an ambiguous place in salvation history. For
Israel, it is often a place of refuge. During a time of famine, the
patriarch Abraham (Abram) took his family there for relief
(see Genesis 12:10). When famine struck again, in the time of
Jacob, the "sons of Israel" went again to Egypt for grain (see
Genesis 42:5). Many centuries later, Jeroboam sought refuge
there when Solomon sought to kill him (1 Kings 11:40), as did
the prophet Uriah in his own time of trouble (Jeremiah 26:21).

Egypt was a place of shelter and asylum, but it also had
dark associations with the most grievous sins. Jacob's sons
had sold their brother Joseph into slavery in Egypt—a sin
that would, in time, lead to the long and brutal enslavement
of their entire nation. It was during their forced labor in Egypt

that many Israelites fell into habits of idolatry, worshipping the gods of Egypt. When at last they were free, they fell again into the worship of the Egyptian bull-god Apis, represented as a golden calf.

Moses delivered the Israelites from slavery in Egypt, and Saint Matthew depicts Jesus as a new and greater Moses, delivering his people from their enslavement to sin.

Both Jesus and Moses had their lives threatened in infancy by an edict to kill male Hebrew children (compare Exodus 1:15–16 with Matthew 2:16). Both Jesus and Moses were saved from the decree by the intervention of a family member (compare Exodus 2:1–10 with Matthew 2:13). Both Jesus and Moses found safety for a while within Egypt (compare Exodus 2:5–10 with Matthew 2:14–15). Both were called back to their respective native lands after a time of hiding (compare Exodus 4:19 with Matthew 2:20). Later in life, both Moses and Jesus spent forty days and nights fasting alone in the desert (Exodus 34:28; Matthew 4:2); and both were commissioned by God to be lawgivers (Deuteronomy 5:1-21; Matthew 5–7).

The exodus event was a landmark event in Israel's history. Its remembrance gave rise to the major feasts of the Jewish calendar, so it was key to the people's identity. Throughout the Bible—the Old Testament and the New Testament—God identified himself repeatedly as the one who brought Israel out of Egypt. The very name of Egypt was used as a synonym for idolatry, oppression, and systemic sin. Even in the

New Testament, the name is symbolic of those who murdered Jesus, God's greatest enemies on earth (see Revelation 11:8).

For the Israelites, Egypt came to represent hell on earth, so for the early Christians the Holy Family's flight into Egypt appears as a "harrowing of hell"—a foreshadowing of what Jesus would accomplish when he opened the gates of heaven to those who had long been dead. We saw in our discussion of the shepherds that with the birth of Jesus, God's glory was no longer confined to the Jerusalem Temple. It now extended to Bethlehem and the shepherds—and even to Egypt and the Egyptians!

The Church Father Saint John Chrysostom said: "Babylon and Egypt represent the whole world. Even when they were engulfed in ungodliness, God signified that he intended to correct and amend both Babylon and Egypt. God wanted humanity to expect his bounteous gifts the world over. So he called from Babylon the wise men and sent to Egypt the Holy Family."[1]

The truth is that colonies of Jews had been thriving in Egypt since the time of the pharaohs. Egypt had been intermittently hospitable to the chosen people, and many Egyptians admired the Israelites' way of life. It was a ruler of Egypt, Ptolemy II, who first commissioned the translation of the

Hebrew Scriptures into Greek. In Egypt the Therapeutae arose and flourished (see our discussion in chapter 5). And it was the Jewish community in Alexandria, Egypt, that produced the singular genius of the philosopher Philo. It is possible that Mary and Joseph had friends—or friends of friends—living in Egypt, among whom they were able to find shelter and support.

We know nothing for certain about those years spent so far from their home. We do know that Christian faith came early to Egypt and has stayed stubbornly through millennia of intense persecution—martyrdom, really—that continues into our own day. Christians in Egypt have always found solace in Saint Matthew's story. As the *Catechism of the Catholic Church* explains: "The flight into Egypt and the massacre of the innocents make manifest the opposition of darkness to the light. . . . Christ's whole life was lived under the sign of persecution. His own share it with him" (CCC 530).

Egypt's native Christians, the Copts, preserve many legends of the Holy Family's sojourn in their land, and they faithfully make pilgrimages to the sites where, according to tradition, the Holy Family found refreshment as they fled. The Copts have also, for centuries, produced a distinctive religious art. In its form it shows the influence of the ancient pharaohs. Its figures are stiff and stylized, rendered in bright primary colors. Yet these Coptic images consistently communicate the life of the Holy Family with overwhelming tenderness, portraying Jesus carried on Joseph's shoulders or cradled at Mary's breast.

The iconography has the quality of memory—and of mercy.

The Babylonian Talmud preserves a story of the exodus—specifically, the moment of Israel's greatest triumph, as the Red Sea closed in upon Pharaoh and his army. The rabbis said: "At that time the ministering angels wanted to chant their hymns before the Holy One, blessed be God, but God said, The work of my hands is being drowned in the sea, and shall you chant hymns before me?"[2]

Among the Proverbs of King Solomon we read: "Do not rejoice when your enemy falls, and let not your heart be glad when he stumbles" (Proverbs 24:17). From the beginning of time, God himself intended the redemption of the Gentiles—even those who, in their ignorance, set themselves against him.

As the Holy Family fled into Egypt, they bore with them the Gospel. It shone through their daily work and domestic life, as long as they remained there. Surely they made many friends for God during their sojourn—friends who were sorry to see them return home after Herod's death. It was as if God were telling them again, this time tenderly: "Israel is my first-born son, and I say to you 'Let my son go that he may serve me'" (see Exodus 4:22–23).

CHAPTER

13

BLESSED TRINITIES: HEAVEN AND THE HOLY FAMILY

S*INCE THE FOURTH CENTURY*, Catholics by the thousands—by the millions—have been going to Sunday Mass and saying the most astonishing things.

I believe in one Lord Jesus Christ,
the Only Begotten Son of God,
born of the Father before all ages.

God from God, Light from Light,
true God from true God,
begotten, not made, consubstantial with the Father;
through him all things were made.
For us men and for our salvation
he came down from heaven,

and by the Holy Spirit was incarnate of the Virgin Mary,
and became man.

We somehow manage to say all of this with the blandest expressions, as if we were reciting a list of active ingredients on a bottle of cough medicine. I know, I know: By this point in the Mass, we've confessed our sins and heard four Bible readings and a homily. Maybe we think we've done enough work for a day of rest. Maybe by this point we're reciting our rote prayers automatically and unthinkingly.

But maybe, too, we fear that we just can't bear the reality of what we're saying.

Maybe we like our God as long as we know he's in heaven, but we fear him when he draws close to us in our sin.

Maybe we fear the truth about Christmas.

Why did God become man? It is one of the great and insolvable mysteries, like Why is there something rather than nothing?

But in this instance an angel gives us a clue by way of the Scriptures. It is the angel who tells Saint Joseph: "You shall call his name Jesus, for he will save his people from their sins" (Matthew 1:21).

Surely Jesus's name, given by heaven, tells us something

about his purpose. He came to "save his people"—more specifically, to save them "from their sins." To do this is a pure act of merciful love, because sins are by definition offenses against almighty God. Yet it is God himself who has taken flesh for the sake of our salvation. He came, moreover, not just to save the wayward members of his chosen people but to save even the gravest sinners of Babylon and Egypt.

In the act of saving us, God drew close to us, so that we could see him and touch him. He became a baby, so that he would need to be picked up and caressed, changed and fed.

As we draw close to God incarnate, we can see more clearly the nature of God eternal. And that, too, was why he became man; revelation is bound up with our salvation. In our fallen state, with our darkened intellect and weakened will, we could not see God or know him, though we could know that he existed.

God drew close so that we could see clearly—and know that "God is love" (1 John 4:8, 16). In eternity, that is his deepest identity. Before he created anything to love, he *was love;* and love is an act that requires both a subject and an object, a lover and a beloved. God *is* that pure act of love. Because of the revelation of Christmas, we know that love as the Blessed Trinity. Pope Saint John Paul II summarized the matter in a memorable way: "God in his deepest mystery is not a solitude, but a family, since he has in himself fatherhood, sonship, and the essence of family, which is love."[1]

It may seem a leap from the manger to the Trinity, but it's not. The dogma of the Trinity appears nowhere explicitly in the infancy narratives, but it is everywhere implied. Christmas is an effusion in time of the love that is eternal—an icon on earth of the love at the heart of heaven. "The glory of the Trinity becomes present in time and space," said Saint John Paul, "and finds its manifestation in Jesus, his Incarnation and his history."[2]

Saint Luke interprets the conception of Christ precisely in the light of the Trinity, as the pope explained. The angel said to Mary: "The Holy Spirit will come upon you, and the power of the Most High will overshadow you; therefore the child to be born will be called holy, the Son of God" (Luke 1:35). Pope Saint John Paul explained this passage:

> The angel's words are like a short Creed which sheds light on the identity of Christ in relation to the other Persons of the Trinity. . . . Christ is the Son of the Most High God, the Great One, the Holy One, the King, the Eternal One, whose conception in the flesh takes place through the power of the Holy Spirit.[3]

In that single line from the angel we encounter God as Father, Son, and Holy Spirit. Nine months later, at Christmas, God manifests himself to the whole world in a deeply personal way—a tri-personal way.

Pope Benedict XVI observed that this startling new revelation was, at the same time, continuous with the Old Testament.

> The angel's words remain entirely within the realm of Old Testament piety, and yet they transcend it. In the light of this new situation, they take on a new realism, a hitherto unforeseeable depth and strength. At this stage, the Trinitarian mystery has not yet been thought through, it has not been worked into a definitive teaching. It appears spontaneously in and through God's way of acting, as prefigured in the Old Testament; it appears within the event, without at this stage becoming a doctrine.[4]

It appears within the event. The Trinity is there for us to ponder, in the details of Christmas.

In our weekly recitation of the Creed we say many curious things. We affirm, for example, that Jesus is "the Only Begotten Son of God, born of the Father before all ages." But what can it mean to be "born" or "begotten" apart from time or sequence? What can it mean for a son to live eternally—simultaneously—with his father? Cardinal Donald Wuerl pondered this mystery in his book of reflections on the Creed:

Jesus is the Only Begotten. He is unique. Only the divine Word is eternally Son in relation to the eternal Father. Their relation is outside time; it is before the beginning. The Father has always been fathering the Son, eternally. This relationship is unique and quite unlike human begetting, which takes place in a sequence of events over the course of time. A human father must precede his son. My father was born in 1909, and in the usual turn of events I was born in 1940. The divine Persons of the Trinity, however, are coeternal. They coexist outside time, and there has never been a moment when one has been without the others.

Thus the term "only begotten" can illuminate God's life for us, but it also challenges us to think beyond ordinary human categories. This is how revelation works. God accommodates himself to us by using our language and even taking on our nature, but he also calls upon us to reach upward to him, to the *super*natural, as he makes us his children and shares the divine nature.[5]

Cardinal Wuerl brings us to an important insight. God was born in time to teach us about his "birth" in eternity. Revelation discloses truth in terms we can understand. To explain the spiritual to us, God draws analogies with what we know. He takes his analogies from the material, physical world.

But at Christmas he is not simply disclosing information. He's not merely dispensing doctrinal data and helping us to understand something that far exceeds our limited minds. *If* that were all he came to do, it would be a wonderful thing. But it's not all. As we've just seen, he also came to save his people from their sins.

But that's still not all! The revelation of Christmas is not merely information, and it's not only about the forgiveness of sins. For God, these are great means to a still mightier end. God *reveals* himself and *forgives* our sins because these are preconditions to a still greater gift, and Cardinal Wuerl touched upon that in the passage we've just read. Salvation consists in God making us his children and sharing his divine nature with us.

The saints have called this the "marvelous exchange." God assumed our human nature in order to give us his divine nature (see 2 Peter 1:4). That is the most profound meaning of our salvation. And Saint Paul put it in terms that evoke the squalor of the stable in Bethlehem: "For you know the grace of our Lord Jesus Christ, that though he was rich, yet for your sake he became poor, so that by his poverty you might become rich" (2 Corinthians 8:9).

Salvation is more than knowledge and more than forgiveness, as great as those gifts are. To be saved is to live like God and to love like God.

We go to Bethlehem because that is where the eternal Father decreed that we should go to meet his eternal Son. We can earn many degrees in theology, but if we do not come to know Jesus as *Son,* we will know little about God. So said the great theologian Joseph Ratzinger (who later became Pope Benedict XVI). Jesus's "existence as a child corresponds in a unique way to his divinity, which is the divinity of the 'Son.' And this means that his existence as a child shows us how we can come to God and to deification."[6]

That's a strong word: *deification.* To be deified is to be made into a god. And that is exactly what God has done for us by sending his Son to Bethlehem. The Son of God became the Son of Man so that we, children of men, might learn how to become children of God. Jesus said: "Unless you turn and become like children, you will never enter the kingdom of heaven" (Matthew 18:3).

Jesus holds many titles. He is King, Savior, Redeemer, Messiah, Lord, Master, Rabbi, and God. But no title is as exalted as Son, and it is as Son that we come to know him at Christmas. Thus, Christmas uniquely shows us the way to salvation. Joseph Ratzinger concluded: "One who has not grasped the mystery of Christmas has failed to grasp the decisive element in Christianity. One who has not accepted this cannot enter the kingdom of heaven."[7]

God wants us with him in the kingdom, and that is why he "sent his Son." The first Christians cherished that phrase for all the love that it implied. For it implies the eternal love of the Trinity as well as its overflow onto the earth. "In this is love," said Saint John, "not that we loved God but that he loved us and *sent his Son* to be the expiation for our sins. . . . And we have seen and testify that the Father has *sent his Son* as the Savior of the world" (1 John 4:10, 14).

Why would God do this? Saint Paul found the answer in Bethlehem: "God *sent forth his Son,* born of woman . . . , to redeem those who were under the law, so that we might receive adoption as sons" (Galatians 4:4–5).

It all comes down to his sonship. And he himself came down to share it, in Bethlehem.

Salvation arrives by way of the family—the Holy Family. The household of Jesus, Mary, and Joseph became a "home away from home" for the eternal Son of God. It was an outpost of heaven, an image of the Trinity in the world. "We may say," said Saint Francis de Sales, "that the Holy Family was a trinity on earth which in a certain way represented the Blessed Trinity itself."[8]

Jesus is, of course, the Son common to both "families." Joseph, in his relationship with Jesus, was an earthly image of the heavenly Father. Mary, who conceived Jesus by the power of the Holy Spirit, became the very image of the Spirit in the world.

So God took his place in a human family—and invited you and me to find our place as well. He made a home for us in the Church, "a people," said Saint Cyprian in the third century, "made one with the unity of the Father, the Son and the Holy Spirit."[9]

And our own homes, too—our Christian homes—also share in this awesome gift of Christmas. Pope Benedict expressed that in the strongest terms I can imagine.

> God had chosen to reveal himself by being born into a human family and the human family thus became an icon of God! God is the Trinity, he is a communion of love; so is the family despite all the differences that exist between the Mystery of God and his human creature, an expression that reflects the unfathomable Mystery of God as Love. . . . The human family, in a certain sense, is an icon of the Trinity because of its interpersonal love and the fruitfulness of this love.[10]

We are created for the sake of love. When we experience love in family life, it is heavenly, but it is still only an image of the greater glory we hope to behold in heaven.

CHAPTER

14

JOY TO THE WORLD!

*J*OY TO THE WORLD!*"* we Christians sing.

And why? Because "The Lord is come!"

If the Lord is our joy, our joy cannot be taken away. It cannot be lost.

In many of the great Christmas entertainments, there are villains who threaten to keep Christmas from coming. The Grinch would steal it away by pilfering its decorations—but the people celebrate anyway. Scrooge would have the day and its humbug be killed off by the sheer force of his stinginess— but he comes to regret his joylessness and lovelessness, and in the end he, too, keeps the festive day.

When it comes to Christmas villains, truth can be far nastier than fiction. For just as surely as there is a historical Saint Nicholas,[1] there are historical scrooges and grinches. The worst of them are the Christian heretics who tried to steal the season's joy by denying the fact of the incarnation.

There were several such killjoys in the early centuries of the Church. Some of them said that Jesus was not really human. Instead, they claimed, he was an angel in disguise—or simply a sort of holographic image projected by God. His feelings were all for show. When he wept, it wasn't from sorrow; he was simply trying to drive home a point. While his body convulsed in pain on the cross, his true self was laughing nearby. Their "Jesus" could be interesting—the way robots and androids in science fiction movies are interesting—but ultimately not lovable. Who could love a deceptive Messiah, a sneering, superior being who moved his drama along by way of manipulation, crocodile tears, and phony rage? And how could we trust that such a liar truly loved us?

Into that camp fell the Gnostics, the Docetists, and others who tried to claim the name "Christian" for a non-incarnational, non-Trinitarian, and ultimately joyless religion.

But there was another camp—a strain of speculation that was, in my opinion, far more corrosive to Christian joy. In that camp were the Adoptionists and Arians, heretics who denied that Jesus was the true God.

Now don't get us wrong—they'd insist—we hold Jesus in great esteem. He was the greatest of God's creatures. But he was only a creature. He was god-ish, because God made him

that way, but he wasn't God the way God is God. He couldn't
be, they'd tell you, because one God who is made up of three
persons is an impossibility. Three does not equal one. And,
anyway, an infinite being could never be contained by a finite
body. Before long, they rationalized their "Jesus" down to
a really nice guy, to whom God had given superpowers at
baptism. Thus, the Feast of the Baptism of the Lord was (after
Easter) their great annual celebration. That feast, they said,
was the anniversary of the Nazarene carpenter's promotion
to demigod and Messiah.

They had little use for Christmas, and even less for Epiphany, because these feasts presented inconvenient data—a
baby boy already identified as God's Son and humanity's
Savior. They wrote anti-Christmas carols, with dismal (but
memorable) refrains that denied Jesus's coequality and co-
eternity with the Father: "There was a time when he was
not," they sang. "There was a time when he was not."

Perhaps we shouldn't be surprised that this heresy—in
its most insidious form, Arianism—took the intellectual
world by storm. In the mid-fourth century, Saint Jerome
complained, "the world groaned and marveled to find itself
Arian." That's how quickly the emperors and academics—
and, sad to say, many bishops—got swept away by the fad.
A few intrepid Christians dared to oppose it. Some of them
chose to die and others to suffer exile and hardship rather

than betray the truth of Christmas. But the idea had powerful advocates, and a few of them were emperors, and that kept the campaign well-funded for a century.

Eventually, however, the Catholic faith triumphed, not because it raised money, or raised an army, but because of Christmas and its characteristic joy.

It's not that Christmas hadn't been on the calendar before. It had indeed, and on different dates in different places. As early as the second century, there were churches in Egypt observing the festival on December 25. The midwinter date coincided with ancient celebrations of Hanukkah, the Jewish Festival of Lights—which, of course, may be no coincidence at all. Some scholars have calculated that date based on details from the account of Zechariah's Temple service in Luke's Gospel.[2]

Elsewhere, Jesus's nativity was kept in remembrance along with other manifestations of his divinity—the visit of the Magi and his first miracle—on the Feast of the Epiphany, on or around January 6.

It was, nevertheless, a relatively quiet celebration, observed the way a parish might keep Trinity Sunday today. Christmas was eclipsed each year by the great primordial Christian festival: Easter.

Feasts, however, take on greater or lesser importance

depending on the circumstances of the Church. And as more people (and more *powerful* people) denied Jesus's true divinity and humanity, Christmas loomed larger. The great Catholic clergy of the fourth century rallied to promote its celebration. Saint Ephrem in Syria and Saint Hilary in Gaul (France) both wrote Christmas carols to serve as antidotes to the catchy hymns produced by the Arians. Saint Gregory of Nazianzus and Saint John Chrysostom urged their congregations to mark the feast with joyful abandon. Saint Augustine in Africa applied his singular rhetorical gifts to the explication of the season's mysteries.

Soon the verdict of history was obvious. The grinches and scrooges had failed to win the hearts of Christians the world over. By the middle of the fifth century, Christmas was a fixture in the Church and on civil calendars; it was the focus of papal preaching; and it was already rising to rival Easter for the cheer it inspired.

Joy had come to the world, and it had come to stay.

Not everyone thinks that the boosting of Christmas's stature has been a good thing. Plenty of people grumble about commercialism, and some complain—on theological grounds—that Christmas should remain more clearly subordinate to Easter, not only in ritual solemnity, but also in terms of the degree of associated revelry. Cardinal Christoph Schönborn took up the question in a recent book.

> If, on the one hand, we start from the Incarnation, when God became man, then it seems to follow that Christmas is the central saving event: God became man! With that, everything has already been fulfilled. Yet is Easter then any more than an appendix? Have redemption and salvation not come to us already, before Easter? On the other hand, Christ's Paschal Mystery does nonetheless seem to be central: Easter is the turning point of salvation, the new thing that makes everything new. Is Easter the noun, then, and Christmas merely the preposition?[3]

So what's it to be? Easter or Christmas? Which holiday should win the hearts of Christians? As often happens, Catholics look at an either-or question and say: both.

The saints, throughout history, have noted that each event is mysteriously linked to the other. In the scenes of Christmas, Christians have always found anticipations of the paschal mystery.

Jesus began his life in a cave used as a stable, and his crib was a stone shelf cut into the wall to make a feeding trough for animals. On the day of his death, too, he was laid on a stone shelf in a tomb.

Those who imagine a manger made of wood observe that

he was laid upon wood at the time of his birth and at the time of his crucifixion.

In birth and in death Jesus would have been wrapped in swaddling bands (compare Luke 2:7 and John 19:40).

Both his birth and his resurrection were announced by angels.

We have already noted the connection between Bethlehem—which means "house of bread"—and Jesus's Last Supper, when he gave his body as the Bread of Life. Lying in the feeding trough, the manger, the baby Jesus was already presenting himself as the "food which endures to eternal life" (John 6:27, 55).

We have already spoken of his circumcision as an anticipation of the bloodshed of his execution. It prefigures his resurrection as well, as a putting off of mortal flesh (see Colossians 2:11).

Christmas, then, poses no threat to Easter's importance. Quite the opposite is true. They are related expressions of the same divine love, ordered one to another by the same Divine Providence.

What Christmas celebrates, on one level, is a revolution in religious thought. Scholars of comparative religions will sometimes try to boil diverse traditions down to a set of motifs

that, stripped of their particularity, begin to look a lot alike—
though rather less like themselves.

It is, moreover, the tendency of polite people in pluralistic
societies to gloss over religious differences and look for common ground. That's a good quality, but it can be taken too
far, and I fear it often is.

For Christianity is singular among the world religions.
Only Christians say that the one true God exists eternally in
a communion of perfect love—that he loves eternally, and he
is loved eternally. Some religions are monotheistic; they pro-
fess belief in one god, as we do—but their god is a solitude.
Other religions are polytheistic; they believe in two gods or
many gods, and inevitably they see their gods as locked in
perpetual strife. These beliefs all lead to distinct moral conse-
quences. They affect life.

Christian faith requires us to believe in love—love
that is stable, eternal, unending, unchanging, undying, supernatural.

Christian faith requires us to believe that eternal love is
interpersonal—tri-personal and triune.

Christian faith requires us to believe that eternal love
broke into history on Christmas Day when God's eternal
"Word became flesh and dwelt among us, full of grace and
truth" (John 1:14). Christian faith compels us to say that
"we have beheld his glory, glory as of the only Son from the
Father" (John 1:14).

The angels sang "Glory" because God's highest glory was touching down on earth, to be shared by the Son with many co-heirs, many brothers and sisters in the "assembly [*ekklesia,* Church] of the firstborn" (Hebrews 12:23). It is in the Church that we celebrate Christmas with saints and innumerable angels in festal gathering, whether we go to Midnight Mass, or Mass at Dawn, or at any time of the blessed day.

Christmas shines uniquely in the world as a beacon of true love. Only Christianity can trace the genealogy of love back infinitely to eternity. Polytheism cannot do this. Nor can monotheism that proposes God as a solitude.

If we do not recognize the difference this makes, we can be sure that the other religions still do. For example, Islam, from its founding, has strongly and fiercely condemned Christianity's doctrines on the Trinity and the incarnation. This condemnation appears in strongest terms in the Koran, and it is engraved upon the walls of the Dome of the Rock.

No human mind could have invented the triune God. He is not a God we can contain in our categories or tame by our thoughts. No human mind could have conceived a God who is love and who loves us as if we were gods. No human mind, unaided by angels, could have dreamt up Christmas.

Christmas makes us different. Christmas sets us apart. Christmas calls us to share in divine love—and then to share that love with an unbelieving world.

That is the summons we have received from the popes in their call for a "New Evangelization." Pope Francis has rightly emphasized "joy" as essential to our task. He titled his letter on evangelization *Evangelii Gaudium*, "The Joy of the Gospel."

> The joy of the gospel fills the hearts and lives of all who encounter Jesus. Those who accept his offer of salvation are set free from sin, sorrow, inner emptiness and loneliness. With Christ joy is constantly born anew.[4]

With Christ, joy is constantly *born anew*. Even the way the pope describes "joy" make us think of Christmas. He makes the connection explicit later in the same letter:

> The joy of the Gospel is for all people: no one can be excluded. That is what the angel proclaimed to the shepherds in Bethlehem: "Be not afraid; for behold, I bring you good news of a great joy which will come to all the people" (Luke 2:10).[5]

God has created the whole world for the sake of the joy we celebrate on Christmas. He fashioned human nature so that every man, woman, and child should desire Christmas joy and seek fulfillment in Bethlehem, the House of Bread—through the Bread that came down from heaven. God made us so that we would find all other joys unsatisfying apart from the joy of Christmas.

He guided all of history for the sake of Christmas joy, calling Abram and leading the old man's descendants, even when they strayed, so that they could find their way back to the road that leads to Bethlehem.

If we truly celebrate Christmas, we'll exude a joy that people will want to share. They'll see the joy in all the holiday traditions we have inherited from our ancestors. Pope Benedict once made a profound study[6] of many of these customs—Christmas trees, Christmas cookies, Christmas gifts—and showed them all to contain profound biblical commentary. The customs themselves express the spiritual insights of ordinary Christians in a memorable, joyful way.

Why do we give gifts? Because God has given himself to us as a gift, wrapping his divinity in true humanity.

Why do we decorate a Christmas tree? To recover the tree of paradise, which was restored by the tree of Calvary. "Then shall all the trees of the wood sing for joy" (Psalm 96:12).

Why do we bake special cookies? Because the Messiah has come to lead us into a land flowing with milk and honey. He has given us "Bread from heaven, having all Sweetness within it."

I believe that Christmas joy is the key to the New Evangelization—and it is deeply Marian, and deeply rooted in our devotion to the Holy Family, the icon of the Trinity on earth.

Such evangelization is for everyone—even those who feel they cannot articulate a defense of the faith, or explain every doctrine, or prove everything from the Bible. Some will go out from Bethlehem as the Magi did, among the elites; some will go out as the shepherds did, among the poor. What both groups shared in common was their joy. They brought Christmas joy from Bethlehem to the world.

We evangelize when we enjoy our Catholic faith—when we enjoy celebrating the feasts—when we have ourselves a merry little Christmas, and invite others to share it. That's the best way to evangelize friends, family, coworkers, and everybody else. Why? Because the world offers countless pleasures, but no lasting joys. What Jesus Christ gives is joy, even in the midst of hardship and sorrow—even amid persecution, flight, and exile.

Joy is the best argument for Catholicism. People find it irresistible and irrefutable. And we have it built into our great feasts. Remember the little poem of Hilaire Belloc:

> *Wherever the Catholic sun doth shine,*
> *There's always laughter and good red wine.*

At least I've always found it so.
Benedicamus Domino!

That's Catholicism, and that's Christmas. Whenever we find ourselves without joy, we should recognize that we ourselves need to be re-evangelized—because the grace of conversion is not something that's ever "over and done"; rather it is ongoing, and ever-deepening, and lifelong.

Even people who don't seem to have a clue about what Christmas is really about will sense a joy at the heart of Christmas. Joy is the reason that stock markets rise and fall on the sale of seasonal gifts and decorations. Christmas commercialism often makes me wince, but I have to admit that it is, in its own way, an acknowledgment of Christmas joy. It's the market's awkward attempt to join the party and capitalize on joy.

Today, as in the fourth century—and as in every century—there are those who would steal our joy by trying to steal our Christmas—by snickering at the lot of it: the Trinity, the virginal conception, the incarnation, the shepherds. How should we respond? By inviting them to the feast. By enjoying the feast ourselves, and by enjoying it for all of its infinite worth.

NOTES

CHAPTER 1: A LIGHT GOES ON IN BETHLEHEM

1. See, for example, John Paul II, *Gratissimam Sane* (letter to Families), February 2, 1994, 23; *Familiaris Consortio* (apostolic exhortation, on the Role of the Christian Family in the Modern World), November 22, 1981, 86; his *Angelus* address on December 26, 1999; and the Holy See's *Charter of the Rights of the Family*, October 22, 1983.

CHAPTER 2: WHAT HAPPENS IN BETHLEHEM . . .

1. St. Justin Martyr, *Dialogue with Trypho* 78; see also 70.
2. Origen, *Against Celsus* 1.51.
3. Pope Benedict XVI, *Jesus of Nazareth: The Infancy Narratives* (New York: Image, 2012), 118.
4. Ibid., 119.
5. Ibid., 17.
6. Ibid., 57.

7. Pope Francis, remarks during meeting with the children of the Italian youth group Azione Cattolica (Catholic Action), December 23, 2013.

CHAPTER 3: A NEW GENESIS

1. See Peter Schäfer, *Jesus in the Talmud* (Princeton, NJ: Princeton University Press, 2007), 15–24. See also Origen, *Against Celsus* 1.28 and 1.32.

2. See the new edition and translation edited by Roger Pearse: *Eusebius of Caesarea: Gospel Problems and Solutions* (Ipswich, UK: Chieftain Publishing, 2010).

CHAPTER 4: THE COUNTERFEIT KINGDOM

1. The New Testament scholar Dale C. Allison Jr. analyzes Dr. King's speeches to make this point in *Scriptural Allusions in the New Testament: Light from the Dead Sea Scrolls* (North Richland Hills, TX: BIBAL Press, 2000), 1–3.

2. On the notion of "messiah" in the Targums for the New Testament, see Craig A. Evans, *From Jesus to the Church: The First Christian Generation* (Louisville: Westminster John Knox, 2014), 39–44; Evans, "Early Messianic Traditions in the Targums," in *Jesus and His Contemporaries: Comparative Studies* (Leiden: Brill, 2001), 155–81; Joseph A. Fitzmyer, *The One Who Is to Come* (Grand Rapids, MI: Eerdmans, 2007), 46–78; Martin McNamara, *Palestinian Judaism and the New Testament* (Wilmington, DE: Michael Glazier, 1983), 205–52; Samson H. Levey, *The Messiah: An Aramaic Interpretation: The Messianic Exegesis of the Targum* (Cincinnati: Hebrew Union College Press/Jewish Institute of Religion, 1974).

3. Macrobius, *Saturnalia* 2.4.11.

4. The passage appears in the Slavonic version of the *Jewish War*

1.370, by the historian Josephus, who was himself a Jew of the first century. It is corroborated in antiquity by the Christian historian Eusebius and by Saint Epiphanius, who probably had access to the source text in Greek.

5. Virgil, Fourth Eclogue, author's translation.

6. Saint Ignatius of Antioch, *Letter to the Ephesians* 19.

CHAPTER 5: MARY: CAUSE OF OUR JOY

1. *Protoevangelium of James* 8, 10.

2. *Apocalypse of Baruch* (2 Baruch) 10.19.

3. See Saint Justin Martyr, *Dialogue with Trypho* 43; and Saint Irenaeus of Lyons, *Adversus Haereses* 3.21. See also Origen, *Contra Celsum* 35.

4. Saint Augustine, *On Virginity* 4.

5. Philo, *Apology* 14.

6. Josephus, *Jewish War* 2.120.

7. Josephus, *Antiquities of the Jews* 18.21.

8. Pliny the Elder, *Natural History* 5.73.

CHAPTER 6: SILENT KNIGHT, HOLY KNIGHT

1. Michael Gasnier, *Joseph the Silent*, trans. Jane Wynne Saul (London: Scepter, 2011).

2. Pope Leo XIII, *Quamquam Pluries* (encyclical, on Devotion to Saint Joseph), August 15, 1889, 4.

3. Maximus of Turin, Sermon 53. For the most comprehensive treatment of the early Church's approaches to Saint Joseph, see Joseph Lienhard, SJ, *St. Joseph in Early Christianity: Devotion and Theology* (Philadelphia: Saint Joseph's University Press, 1999).

4. Pseudo-Origen, Homily 17. See Lienhard, *St. Joseph in Early Christianity*, p. 20.

5. Saint Jerome, *Against Helvidius* 6.

6. Pope Benedict XVI, address at the Basilica of Marie, Reine des Apôtres in the Mvolyé neighborhood—Yaoundé, Cameroon, March 18, 2009.

CHAPTER 7: ANGELS: ECHOING THEIR JOYOUS STRAINS

1. In discussing the holy angels I'm drawing from years of long conversations with my friend Mike Aquilina and from my close reading of his books: *Angels of God: The Bible, the Church, and the Heavenly Hosts* (Ann Arbor, MI: Servant Books, 2009); *A Year with the Angels: Daily Meditations with the Messengers of God* (Charlotte, NC: Saint Benedict Press, 2011); and *Entertaining Angels* (Charlotte, NC: Catholic Scripture Study International, 2013).
2. Billy Graham, *Angels: Ringing Assurance That We Are Not Alone* (Nashville: Thomas Nelson, 1995), 23.

CHAPTER 8: O LITTLE TOWN OF BETHLEHEM

1. Pseudonymous *Psalms of Solomon* 17: 23-29.
2. Eusebius of Caesarea, *Church History* 3.20.
3. Jerome Murphy-O'Connor, OP, "Where Was Jesus Born?" in *Bible Review,* February 2000, 54.

CHAPTER 9: DO YOU BELIEVE IN MAGI?

1. Pliny the Elder, *Natural History* 30.1–2.
2. Ibid.
3. Origen, *Contra Celsum* 1.60. See also Saint Irenaeus of Lyons, *Against the Heresies* 3.9.2.
4. Saint Ephrem of Syria, *Hymns on the Nativity* 15.29.
5. Saint Ephrem the Deacon, *Hymns on the Nativity* 14.11.

6. Saint John Chrysostom, *Homilies on the Gospel of Matthew* 6.3.
7. Philo of Alexandria, *De Plantatione*.
8. Pope Saint Gregory the Great, *Homily on Epiphany* (Tenth Homily on the Gospels).

CHAPTER 10: SHEPHERDS, WHY THIS JUBILEE?

1. *The Book of the Popes (Liber Pontificalis)*, trans. Louise Ropes Loomis (New York: Columbia University Press, 1916), 12–13.

CHAPTER 11: THE GLORY OF YOUR PEOPLE: THE PRESENTATION

1. I discuss the scene of the presentation—and its relation to the prescriptions of Exodus 13—in great detail in my book *Kinship by Covenant: A Canonical Approach to the Fulfillment of God's Saving Promises* (New Haven, CT: Yale Anchor Bible Reference Library, 2009), 166–72.
2. Note Luke's description of Jesus as the firstborn of Mary in Luke 2:7, and commentary by Joseph A. Fitzmyer, *The Gospel According to Luke I–IX*, Anchor Bible series, vol. 28 (Garden City, NY: Doubleday, 1980), 407.
3. See Father Pablo Gadenz, "The Priest as Spiritual Father," in *Catholic for a Reason: Scripture and the Mystery of the Family of God*, ed. Scott Hahn and Leon Suprenant (Steubenville, OH: Emmaus Road Publishing, 1998), 228–29.
4. Charles H. Talbert, *Reading Luke: A Literary and Theological Commentary on the Third Gospel* (New York: Crossroad, 1989), 36. See also B. Reicke, "Jesus, Simeon, and Anna (Luke 2:21-40)," in *Saved by Hope: Essays in Honor of Richard C. Oudersluys*, ed. J. I. Cook (Grand Rapids, MI: Eerdmans, 1978), 100.
5. See H. D. Park, *Finding* Herem? *A Study of Luke-Acts in the Light of* Herem, Library of New Testament Studies, vol. 357 (New York: T&T Clark, 2007), 160.

6. See Jon D. Levenson, *Theology of the Program of Restoration of Ezekiel* (Missoula, MN: Scholars Press, 1976), 40–48, 150: "The theology of the Epistle to the Hebrews presents Jesus as the heir to both eternal covenants, the Davidic and the Priestly."
7. For a discussion of Scripture as "defiling the hands," see James D. G. Dunn, ed., *Jews and Christians: The Parting of the Ways, A.D. 70 to 135* (Grand Rapids, MI: Eerdmans, 1999), 12f.

CHAPTER 12: FLIGHT INTO JOY

1. Saint John Chrysostom, *Homilies on the Gospel of Matthew* 8.2.
2. Babylonian Talmud, *Tractate Megillah* 10B.

CHAPTER 13: BLESSED TRINITIES: HEAVEN AND THE HOLY FAMILY

1. Pope John Paul II, *Puebla: A Pilgrimage of Faith* (Boston: Daughters of St. Paul, 1979), 86.
2. Pope John Paul II, General audience, April 5, 2000, 2.
3. Ibid., 3.
4. Pope Benedict XVI, *Jesus of Nazareth: The Infancy Narratives* (New York: Image, 2012), 29–30.
5. Cardinal Donald Wuerl, *Faith That Transforms Us: Reflections on the Creed* (Frederick, MD: Word Among Us, 2013), 31–32.
6. Joseph Ratzinger, *The Blessing of Christmas* (San Francisco: Ignatius Press, 2007), 76.
7. Ibid.
8. Saint Francis de Sales, *Discourses* 19.
9. Saint Cyprian of Carthage, *On the Lord's Prayer* 23.
10. Pope Benedict XVI, *Angelus*, December 27, 2009.